MILITARY HISTORY OF BELGIUM DURING WORLD WAR II

Books LLC®, Reference Series, Memphis, USA, 2011. ISBN: 9781156131701. www.booksllc.net. Copyright: http://creativecommons.org/licenses/by-sa/3.0/deed.en

Table of Contents

Battles and operations of World War II involving Belgium
Battle of Belgium 1
Battle of Belgium (1940) order of battle 15
Battle of Fort Eben-Emael 17
Battle of Hannut 22
Battle of the Scheldt 28

Belgian Resistance
Belgian Resistance 32
Comet line 33

Comité de Défense des Juifs 34
Free Belgian Forces 35
Front de l'Indépendance 36
Nazi Ghost Train 37
Robert Jan Verbelen 37
Todor Angelov 38
Twentieth convoy 39
Wallonie Libre 40
William Herskovic 40
Österreichische Freiheitsfront 41

Military history of Belgium during World War II
1st Belgian Infantry Brigade 42
Fort Eben-Emael 43
KW-line 45

Military units and formations of Belgium in World War II
349th Squadron (Belgium) 45
350th Squadron (Belgium) 46
5th Special Air Service 46
No. 10 (Inter-Allied) Commando 47

Introduction

Purchase of this book entitles you to a free trial membership in the publisher's book club at www.booksllc.net. (Time limited offer.) Simply enter the barcode number from the back cover onto the membership form. The book club entitles you to select from hundreds of thousands of books at no additional charge. You can also download a digital copy of this and related books to read on the go. Simply enter the title or subject onto the search form to find them.

Each chapter in this book ends with a URL to a hyperlinked online version. Type the URL exactly as it appears. If you change the URL's capitalization it won't work. Use the online version to access related pages, websites, footnotes, tables, color photos, updates. Click the version history tab to see the chapter's contributors. Click the edit link to suggest changes.

A large and diverse editor base collaboratively wrote the book, not a single author. After a long process of discussion and debate, the chapters gradually took on a neutral point of view reached through consensus. Additional editors expanded and contributed to chapters striving to achieve balance and comprehensive coverage. This reduced the regional or cultural bias found in many other books and provided access and breadth on subject matter otherwise little documented.

Battle of Belgium

The **Battle of Belgium** or **Belgian Campaign** formed part of the greater Battle of France, an offensive campaign by Germany during the Second World War. It took place over 18 days in May 1940 and ended with the German occupation of Belgium following the surrender of the Belgian Army.

On 10 May 1940, Germany's armed forces, the *Wehrmacht*, invaded Luxembourg, The Netherlands, and Belgium under the operational plan *Fall Gelb* (Case Yellow). The Allied Armies attempted to halt the German Army in Belgium, believing it to be the main German thrust. After the French had fully committed the best of the Allied Armies to Belgium between 10 and 12 May, the Germans enacted the second phase of their operation, a breakthrough, or sickle cut, through the Ardennes, and advanced towards the English Channel. The German Army (*Heer*) reached the Channel after five days, encircling the Allied Armies. The Germans gradually reduced the pocket of Allied forces, forcing them back to the sea. The Belgian Army surrendered on 28 May 1940, ending the battle.

The Battle of Belgium included the first tank battle of the war, the Battle of Hannut. It was the largest tank battle in history up to that date but was later surpassed by the battles of the North African campaign and the Eastern Front. The battle also included the Battle of Fort Eben-Emael, the first strategic airborne operation using paratroopers.

The German official history stated that in the 18 days of bitter fighting, the Belgian Army were tough opponents, and spoke of the "extraordinary bravery" of its soldiers. The Belgian collapse forced the Allied withdrawal from continental Europe. The British Royal Navy evacuated Belgian ports during Operation Dynamo, allowing the British Army to escape and continue military operations. Belgium was occupied by the Germans until the winter of 1944–1945, when it was liberated by the Western Alliance.

Pre-battle plans

Belgium's strained alliances

The Belgian strategy for a defence against German aggression faced political as well military problems. In terms of military strategy, the Belgians were unwilling to stake everything on a linear defence of the Belgian–German border, in an extension of the Maginot Line. Such a move would leave the Belgians vulnerable to a German assault in their rear, through an attack on the Netherlands. Such a strategy would also rely on the French to move quickly into Belgium and support the garrison there. Politically, the Belgians did not trust the French. Marshal Philippe Pétain had suggested a French strike at Germany's Ruhr area using Belgium as a springboard in October 1930 and again in January 1933. Belgium feared it would be drawn into a war regardless, and sought to avoid that eventuality. The Belgians also feared being drawn into a war as a result of the French–Soviet pact of May 1935. The Franco-Belgian agreement stipulated Belgium was to mobilise if the Germans did, but what was not clear was if Belgium would have to mobilise in the event of a German invasion of Poland.

The Belgians much preferred an alliance with Great Britain. The British had entered the First World War in response to the German violation of Belgian neutrality. The Belgian Channel ports had offered the German Imperial Navy valuable bases, and such an attack would offer the German *Kriegsmarine* and the *Luftwaffe* bases to engage in strategic offensive operations against the United Kingdom in the coming conflict. But the British government paid little attention to the concerns of the Belgians. The lack of this commitment ensured the Belgian withdrawal from the Western Alliance, the day before the German re-occupation of the Rhineland. The German remilitarisation of the Rhineland served to convince the Belgians that France and Britain were unwilling to fight for their own strategic interests, let alone Belgium's. The Belgian General Staff was determined to fight for its own interests, alone if necessary.

The Belgian place in Allied strategy

The French were infuriated at King Leopold III's open declaration of neutrality in October 1936. The French Army saw its strategic assumptions undermined; it could no longer expect closer cooperation with the Belgians in defending the latter's eastern borders, enabling a German attack to be checked well forward of the French border. The French were dependent on how much cooperation they could extract from the Belgians. Such a situation deprived the French any prepared defences in Belgium to forestall an attack, a situation which the French had wanted to avoid as it meant engaging the German Panzer Divisions in a mobile battle. The French considered invading Belgium immediately in response to a German attack on the country. Nevertheless the Belgians, recognising the danger posed by the Germans, secretly made their own defence policies, troop movement information, communications, fixed defence dispositions, intelligence and air reconnaissance arrangements available to the French military attaché in Brussels.

The Allied plan to aid Belgium was the Dyle Plan; the cream of the Allied forces, which included the French Armoured divisions, would advance to the Dyle river in response to a German invasion. The choice of an established Allied line lay in either reinforcing the Belgians in the east of the country, at the Meuse–Albert Canal line, and holding the Scheldt Estuary, thus linking the French defences in the south with the Belgian forces protecting Ghent and Antwerp, seemed to be the soundest defensive strategy. The weakness of the plan was that, politically at least, it abandoned most of eastern Belgium to the Germans. Militarily it would put the Allied rear at right angles to the French frontier defences; while for the British, their communications located at the Bay of Biscay ports, would be parallel to their front. Despite the risk of committing forces to central Belgium and an advance to the Schedlt or Dyle lines, which would be vulnerable to an outflanking move, Maurice Gamelin, the French commander, approved the plan and it remained the Allied strategy upon the outbreak of war.

The British, with no army in the field and behind in rearmament, was in no position to challenge French strategy, which had assumed the prominent role of the Western Alliance. Having little ability to oppose the French, the British strategy for military action came in the form of strategic bombing of the Ruhr industry.

Belgian military strategy

(future) King Leopold III (left), with King Albert I

Upon the official Belgian withdrawal from the Western Alliance, the Belgians refused to engage in any official staff meetings with the French or British military staff for fear of compromising its neutrality. The Belgians did not regard a German invasion as inevitable and were determined that if an invasion did take place it would be effectively resisted by new fortifications such as Eben Emael. The Belgians had taken measures to reconstruct their defences along the border with the German state upon Adolf Hitler's rise to power in January 1933. The Belgian government had watched with increasing alarm the German withdrawal from the League of Nations, its repudiation of the Treaty of Versailles and its violation of the Locarno Treaties. The government increased expenditure on modernising the fortifications at Namur and Liège. New lines of defence were established along the Maastricht–Bois-le-Duc canal, joining the Meuse, Scheldt and the Albert Canal. The protection of the eastern frontier, based mainly on the destruction of a number of roads, was entrusted to new formations (frontier cyclist units, "*Chasseurs Ardennais*"). By 1935, the Belgian defences had been completed. Even so, it was felt that the defences were no longer adequate. A significant mobile reserve was needed to guard the rear areas, and as a result it was considered that the protection against a sudden assault by German forces was not sufficient. Significant manpower reserves were also needed, but a bill made for the provision of longer military service and training for the army, was rejected by the public on the basis that it would increase Belgium's military commitments as well as the request of the Allies to engage in conflicts far from home.

King Leopold III made a speech on 14 October 1936 in front of the Council of Ministers, in an attempt to persuade the people (and its Government) the defences needed strengthening. He outlined three main military points for Belgium's increased rearmament:

a) German rearmament, following upon the complete remilitarization of Italy and Russia (the Soviet Union), caused most other states, even those that were deliberately pacific, like Switzerland and the Netherlands, to take exceptional precautions.

b) There has been such a vast change in the methods of warfare as a result of technical progress, particularly in aviation and mechanisation, that the initial operations of armed conflict could now be of such force, speed and magnitude as to be particularly alarming to small countries like Belgium.

c) Our anxieties have been increased by the lightning reoccupation of the Rhineland and the fact that bases for the start of a possible German invasion have been moved near to our frontier.

On 24 April 1937, the French and British delivered a public declaration that Belgium's security was paramount to the Western Allies and that they would defend their frontiers accordingly against aggression of any sort, whether this aggression was directed solely at Belgium, or as a means of obtaining bases from which to wage war against "other states". The British and French, under those circumstances, released Belgium from her Locarno obligations to render mutual assistance in the event of German aggression toward Poland, while the British and French maintained their military obligations to Belgium.

Militarily, the Belgians considered the *Wehrmacht* to be stronger than the Allies, particular the British Army and engaging in overtures to the Allies would result in Belgium becoming a battleground without adequate Allies. The Belgians and French remained confused about what was expected of each other if or when, hostilities commenced. The Belgians were determined to hold the border fortifications along the Albert Canal and the Meuse, without withdrawing, until the French Army arrived to support them. Gamelin was not keen on pushing his Dyle plan that far. He was concerned that the Belgians would be driven out of their defences and would retreat to Antwerp, as in 1914. In fact, the Belgian divisions protecting the border were to withdraw and retreat southward to link up with French forces. This information was not given to Gamelin. As far as the Belgians were concerned, the Dyle Plan had advantages. Instead of the limited Allied advance to the Scheldt, or meeting the Germans on the Franco-Belgian border, the move to the Dyle river would reduce the Allied front in central Belgium by 70 kilometres (43 mi), freeing more forces for use as a strategic reserve. It was felt it would save more Belgian territory, in particular the eastern industrial regions. It also had the advantage of absorbing Dutch and Belgian Army formations (including some 20 Belgian divisions). Gamelin was to justify the Dyle Plan after the defeat using these arguments.

On 10 January 1940, in an episode known as the Mechelen Incident, a German Army Major Hellmuth Reinberger crash-landed in a Messerschmitt Bf 108 near Mechelen-sur-Meuse. Reinberger was carrying the first plans for the German invasion of western Europe which, as Gamelin had expected, entailed a repeat of the 1914 Schlieffen Plan and a German thrust through the Belgium (which was expanded by the **Wehrmacht** to include the Netherlands) and into France. The plan was nothing more than a land grab to occupy the low countries as a base to conduct naval, aerial and ground offensives.

The Belgians suspected a ruse, but the plans were taken seriously. Belgian intelligence and the military attaché in Cologne correctly suggested the Germans would not commence the invasion with this plan. It suggested that the Germans would try an attack through the Belgian Ardennes and advance to Calais with the aim of encircling the Allied armies in Belgium. The Belgians had correctly predicted the Germans would attempt a *Kesselschlacht* (direct translation: "Cauldron battle", meaning encirclement battle), to destroy its enemies. The Belgians had predicted the exact German plan as offered by Erich von Manstein.

The Belgian High Command warned the French and British of their concerns. They feared that the Dyle plan would put not just the Belgian strategic position in danger, but also the entire left wing of the Allied front. King Leopold and General Raoul Van Overstraeten, the King's *Aide de Camp*, warned Gamelin and the French Army Command of their concerns on 8 March and 14 April. They were ignored.

4 - Battle of Belgium

Belgian plans for defensive operations

Eben-Emael: the Belgians hoped to severely delay the Germans using such fortifications

The Belgian plan, *in the event of German aggression* [italics in original] provided for:
(a) A delaying position along the Albert Canal from Antwerp to Liege and the Meuse from Liege to Namur, which was to be held long enough to allow French and British troops to occupy the line Antwerp–Namur–Givet. It was anticipated that the forces of the guarantor Powers would be in action on the third day of an invasion.
(b) Withdrawal to the Antwerp–Namur position.
(c) The Belgian Army was to hold the sector–excluding Leuven, but including Antwerp–as part of the main Allied defensive position.
In an agreement with the British and French Armies, the French 7th Army under the command of Henri Giraud was to advance into Belgium, past the Scheldt Estuary in Zeeland if possible, to Breda, in the Netherlands. The British Army's British Expeditionary Force or B.E.F, commanded by General Lord Gort, was to occupy the central position in the Brussels–Ghent gap supporting the Belgian Army holding the main defensive positions some 20 kilometres (12 mi) east of Brussels. The main defensive position ringing Antwerp would be protected by the Belgians, barely 10 kilometres (6.2 mi) from the city. The French 7th Army was to reach the Zeeland or Breda, just inside the Dutch border. The French would then be in a position to protect the left flank of the Belgian Army forces protecting Antwerp and threaten the German northern flank.

Further east, delaying positions were constructed in the immediate tactical zones along the Albert Canal, which joined with the defences of the Meuse west of Maastricht. The line deviated southward, and continued to Liege. The Maastricht–Liege gap was heavily protected. Fort Eben-Emael guarded the city's northern flank, the tank country lying in the strategic depths of the Belgian forces occupying the city and the axis of advance into the west of the country. Further lines of defence ran south west, covering the Liege–Namur axis. The Belgian Army also had the added benefit of the French 1st Army, advancing toward Gembloux and Hannut, on the southern flank of the B.E.F and covering the Sambre sector. This covered the gap in the Belgian defences between the main Belgian positions on the Dyle line with Naumr to the south. Further south still, the French 9th Army advanced to the Givet–Dinat axis on the Meuse river. The French 2nd Army was responsible for the last 100 kilometres (62 mi) of front, covering Sedan, the lower Meuse, the Belgian–Luxembourg border and the northern flank of the Maginot line.

German operational plans

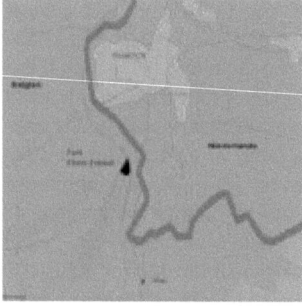

Map of the area between Belgium and the Netherlands near Fort Eben-Emael: The fort protected the vital strategic bridgeheads into Belgium

The German plan of attack required that Army Group B would advance and draw in the Allied First Army Group into central Belgium, while Army Group A conducted the surprise assault through the Ardennes. Belgium was to act as a secondary front with regard to importance. Army Group B was given only limited numbers of armoured and mobile units while the vast majority of the Army Group comprised infantry divisions. After the English Channel was reached, all Panzer division units and most Motorised infantry were removed from Army Group B and given to Army Group A, to strengthen the German lines of communication and to prevent an Allied breakout. Such a plan would still fail if sufficient ground could not be taken quickly in Belgium to squeeze the allies against two fronts. Preventing this from happening were the defences of Fort Eben-Emael and the Albert Canal. The three bridges over the canal were the key to allowing Army Group B a high operational tempo. The bridges at Veldwezelt, Vroenhoven and Kanne in Belgium, and Maastricht on the Dutch border were the target. Failure to capture the bridges would leave Reichenau's German 6th Army, the southern-most army of Group B, trapped in the Maastricht-Albert Canal enclave and subjected to the fire of Eben-Emael. The fort had to be captured or destroyed.

Adolf Hitler summoned Lieutenant-General Kurt Student of the *7. Flieger-Division* (7th Air Division) to discuss the assault. It was first suggested that a conventional parachute drop be made by airborne forces to seize and destroy the forts' guns before the land units approached. Such a suggestion was rejected as the Junkers Ju 52 transports were too slow and were likely to be vulnerable to Dutch and Belgian anti-aircraft guns. Other factors for its refusal were the weather conditions, which might blow the paratroopers away from the fort and disperse them too widely. A seven-second drop from a Ju 52 at minimum operational height led to a dispersion over 300 metres alone.

Hitler had noticed one potential flaw in the defences. The roofs were flat and unprotected; he demanded to know if a glider, such as the DFS 230, could land on them. Student replied that it could be done, but only by 12 aircraft and in daylight; this would deliver 80–90 paratroopers onto the target. Hitler then revealed the tactical weapon that would make this strategic operation work, introducing the *Hohlladungwaffe* (hollow-charge) – a 50 kilograms (110 lb) explosive weapon which would destroy the Belgian gun emplacements. It was this tactical unit that would spearhead the first strategic airborne operation in history.

Forces involved

Belgian forces

The Belgian Army could muster 22 Divisions, which contained 1,338 artillery pieces but just 10 tanks. The Belgians began mobilisation on 25 August 1939 and by May 1940 mounted a field army of 18 infantry divisions, two divisions of Chasseurs Ardennais (partly motorised) and two motorised cavalry divisions, a force totalling some 600,000 men. Belgian reserves may have been able to field 900,000 men. The army lacked armour and anti-aircraft guns. After the completion of the Belgian Army's mobilisation, it could muster five Regular Corps and two reserve Army Corps consisting of 12 regular infantry divisions, two divisions of Chasseurs Ardennais, six reserve infantry divisions, one Brigade of Cyclist Frontier Guards, one Cavalry Corps of two divisions and one Brigade of motorised cavalry. The Army contained two anti-aircraft artillery and four Army artillery regiments and an unknown quantity of fortress, engineer and signals force personnel.

The Belgian Naval Corps was resurrected in 1939. Most of the Belgian Merchant fleet, of some 100 ships, evaded capture by the Germans. Under the terms of a Belgian–Royal Navy agreement these ships, and the 3,350 sailors and crew, were placed under British control for the duration of hostilities. The General headquarters of the Belgian Admiralty were based at Ostend under the command of Major Henry Decarpentrie. The First Naval Division was based at Ostend, while the second and third divisions were based at Zeebrugge and Antwerp.

A Fairey Fox of the Aéronautique Militaire Belge

The Aéronautique Militaire Belge (AéMI), the Belgian Air Force, had barely begun to modernise their aircraft technology. They had ordered the Brewster Buffalo, Fiat CR.42, Hawker Hurricane, Koolhoven F.K.56, Fairey Battle, Caproni Ca.312 light bombers and Caproni Ca.335 fighter-reconnaissance aircraft. Only the Fiats, Hurricanes and Battles had been delivered. The shortage of modern types meant single-seat versions of the Fairey Fox light bomber were being used as fighters. The AéMI possessed 250 combat aircraft. At least 90 were fighter aircraft, 12 were bombers and 12 were reconnaissance aircraft. Only 50 were of reasonably modern standard. When including liaison and transport aircraft from all services are added, a total strength of 377 is reached; however only 118 of these were serviceable on 10 May 1940. Of this number around 78 fighters and 40 bombers were operational. The AéMI was put under the command of Paul Hiernaux, who had received his pilot's licence just before the outbreak of the First World War, and had risen to the position of Commander-in-Chief in 1938. Hiernaux organised the service into three air regiments; the first (1er Régiment d'Aéronautique), which contained 60 aircraft, the second (2e Régiment d'Aéronautique), comprising 53 aircraft and the third (3e Régiment d'Aéronautique), with a further 79 machines.

French forces

The Belgians were afforded substantial support by the French Army. The French 1st Army comprised General René Prioux's Cavalry Corps. The Corps was given the 2nd Light Mechanised Division (2e Division Légère Mécanique, or 2e DLM) and the 3rd Light Mechanised Division (3e DLM) which were allocated to defend the Gembloux gap. The armoured forces consisted of 176 of the formidable SOMUA S35s and 239 Hotchkiss H35 light tanks. Both of these types, in armour and firepower, were superior to most German types. The 3e DLM contained 90 S35s and some 140 H35s alone. The French 7th Army was to protect the northernmost part of the Allied front. Containing the 1st Light Mechanised Division (1e DLM), the 25th Motorised Division and the 9th Motorised Division. This force would advance to Breda in the Netherlands.

The third French army to see action on Belgian soil was the 9th. It was weaker than both the 7th and particularly the French 1st Armies. The 9th Army was allocated infantry divisions with the exception of the 5th Motorised Division. The 9th Army's mission was to protect the southern flank of the Allied armies, south of the Sambre river and just north of Sedan. Further south lay the French 2nd Army, in France protecting the Franco-Belgian border between Sedan and Montmédy. The two weakest French armies were protecting the area of the main German thrust.

British forces

The British contributed the weakest force to Belgium. The B.E.F, under the command of General Lord Gort VC, consisted of just 152,000 men in two Corps of two divisions each. It was hoped to field two armies of two Corps each, but this scale of mobilisation never took place. The I Corps was commanded by Lt-Gen. John Dill, later Lt-Gen. Michael Barker, who was in turn replaced by Major-General Harold

Alexander. Lt-Gen. Alan Brooke commanded II Corps. Later the III Corps under Lt-Gen. Ronald Adam was added to the British order of battle. A further 9,392 Royal Air Force (RAF) personnel of the RAF Advanced Air Striking Force under the command of Air Vice-Marshal Patrick Playfair was to support operations in Belgium. By May 1940 the B.E.F had grown to 394,165 men, of whom more than 150,000 were part of the logistical rear area organisations and had little military training. On 10 May 1940, the B.E.F comprised just 10 divisions (not all at full strength), 1,280 artillery pieces and 310 tanks.

German forces
Army Group B was placed under the command of Fedor von Bock. It was allocated 26 infantry and three Panzer divisions for the invasion of the Netherlands and Belgium. Of the three Panzer Divisions, the 3rd and 4th were to operate in Belgium under the command of the 6th Army's XVI Corps. The 9th Panzer Division was attached to the 18th Army which, after the Battle of the Netherlands, would support the push into Belgium alongside the 18th Army and cover its northern flank. German armour strength in Army Group B amounted to 808 tanks, of which 282 were Panzer Is, 288 were Panzer IIs, 123 were Panzer IIIs and 66 were Panzer IVs; 49 command tanks were also operational. The 3rd Panzer Division's armoured regiments consisted of 117 Panzer Is, 128 Panzer IIs, 42 Panzer IIIs, 26 Panzer IVs and 27 command tanks. The 4th Panzer Division had 136 Panzer Is, 105 Panzer IIs, 40 Panzer IIIs, 24 Panzer IVs and 10 command tanks. The 9th Panzer, scheduled initially for operations in the Netherlands, was the weakest division with only 30, 54, 123, 66 and 49 of the respective types. The elements of the 7th Air Division and the 22nd Airlanding Division, that were to take part in the attack on Fort Eben-Emael, were named *Sturmabteilung Koch* (Assault Detachment Koch); named after the commanding officer of the group, Hauptmann Walter Koch. The force was assembled in November 1939. It was primarily composed of parachutists from the 1st Parachute Regiment and engineers from the 7th Air Division, as well as a small group of *Luftwaffe* pilots.

The *Luftwaffe* allocated 1,815 combat, 487 transport aircraft and 50 gliders for the assault on the Low Countries. The initial air strikes over Belgian air space were to be conducted by *IV. Fliegerkorps* under *General der Flieger Generaloberst* Alfred Keller. Keller's force consisted of *Lehrgeschwader 1* (Stab. I., II., III., IV.), *Kampfgeschwader 30* (Stab. I., II., III.) and *Kampfgeschwader 27* (III.). On 10 May Keller had 363 aircraft (224 serviceable) augmented by *Generalmajor* Wolfram von Richthofen's *VIII. Fliegerkorps* with 550 (420 serviceable) aircraft. They in turn were supported by *Oberst* Kurt-Bertram von Döring's *Jagdfliegerführer 2*, with 462 fighters (313 serviceable).

Keller's *IV. Fliegerkorps* headquarters would operate from Düsseldorf, LG 1. KG 30 which was based at Oldenburg and its III. Gruppe were based at Marx. Support for Döring and Von Richthofen came from North Rhine-Westphalia and bases in Grevenbroich, Mönchengladbach, Dortmund and Essen.

Battle
10–11 May: The border Battles
During the evening of 9 May, the Belgian Military attaché in Berlin intimated that the Germans intended to attack the following day. Offensive movement of enemy forces were detected on the border. At 00:10 on 10 May 1940, at General Headquarters an unspecified squadron in Brussels gave the alarm. A full state of alert was instigated at 01:30 am. Belgian forces took up their deployment positions.

At roughly 04:00, the first air raids were conducted against airfields and communication centres. The Allied armies had enacted their Dyle plan on the morning of 10 May, and were approaching the Belgian rear. King Leopold had gone to his Headquarters near Briedgen, Antwerp. The *Luftwaffe* was to spearhead the aerial battle in the low countries. Its first task was the elimination of the Belgian air contingent. Despite an overwhelming numerical superiority of 1,375 aircraft, 957 of which were serviceable, the air campaign in Belgium had limited success overall. It still had a tremendous impact on the AéMI, which had only 179 aircraft on 10 May.

The victors of Eben-Emael: *Fallschirmjäger* of Sturmabteilung Koch

Much of the success was down to Richthofen's subordinates, particularly KG 77 and its commander *Oberst* Dr. Johann-Volkmar Fisser whose attachment to VIII. Fliegerkorps, was noted by *Generalmajor* Wilhelm Speidel, he commented "...was the result of the well-known tendency of the commanding general to conduct his own private war". Fisser's KG 77 destroyed the AéMI main bases, with help from KG 54. Fighters from JG 27 eliminated two squadrons at Neerhepsen, and during the afternoon, I./St.G 2 destroyed nine of the 15 Fiat CR.42 fighters at Brusthem. The only other success was KG 27s destruction of eight aircraft at Belesle. A total of 83 machines–mostly trainers and "squadron hacks", were destroyed. The AéMI flew only 146 sorties in the first six days. Between 16 May and 28 May, the AéMI flew just 77 operations. It spent most of its time retreating and fuel withdrawing in the face of *Luftwaffe* attacks.

The German planners had recognised the need to eliminate Fort Eben-Emael if it was to break into the interior of Belgium. It decided to deploy airborne forces (*Fallschirmjäger*) to land inside the fortress perimeter using gliders. Using special explosives (and flamethrowers) to disable the defences, the *Fallschirmjäger* then entered the fortress. In the ensuing battle, German infantry overcame the defenders of the I Belgian Corps' 7th Infantry Division in 24 hours. The main Belgian defence line had been breached and German infantry of the 18th Army had passed through it rapidly. Moreover, German soldiers had established bridgeheads across the Albert Canal before the British were able to reach it some 48 hours later. The Chasseurs Ardennais further south, on the orders of their commander, withdrew behind the Meuse, destroying some bridges in their wake.

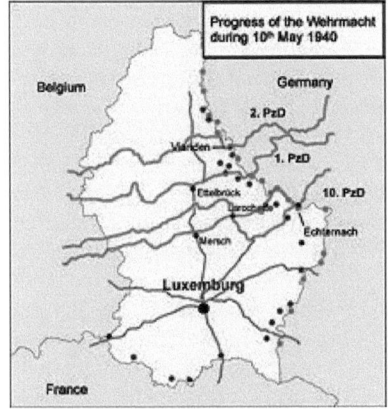

Operation Niwi was designed to ease the route of the Panzer Divisions through the Luxembourg–Belgian routes

Further successful German airborne offensive operations were carried out in Luxembourg which seized five crossings and communication routes leading into France. The offensive, carried out by 125 volunteers of the 34th Infantry Division under the command of Wenner Hedderich, achieved their missions by flying to their objectives using Fieseler Fi 156 *Störche*. The cost was the loss of five aircraft and 30 dead. With the fort breached, the Belgian 4th and 7th Infantry Divisions were confronted by the prospect of fighting an enemy on relatively sound terrain (for armour operations). The 7th Division, with its 2nd and 18th Grenadier Regiments and 2nd Carabineers, struggled to hold their positions and contain the German infantry on the west bank. The Belgian tactical units engaged in several counterattacks. At one point, at Briedgen, they succeeded in retaking the bridge and blowing it up. At the other points, Vroenhoven and Veldwezeltz, the Germans had had time to establish strong bridgeheads and repulsed the attacks.

A little known third airborne operation, Operation Niwi, was also conducted on 10 May in southern Belgium. The objectives of this operation was to land two companies of the 3rd battalion Großdeutschland Infantry Regiment by Fi 156 aircraft at Nives and Witry in the south of the country, in order to clear a path for the 1st and 2nd Panzer divisions which were advancing through the Belgian–Luxembourg Ardennes. The original plan called for the use of Junkers Ju 52 transport aircraft, but the short landing run (27 metres) capability of the Fi 156 saw 200 of these aircraft used in the assault. The operational mission was to:
1. Cut signal communications and message links on the Neufchâteau–Bastogne and Neufchâteau–Martelange roads. [Neufchâteau being the largest southern-most city in Belgium]
2. Prevent the approach of reserves from the Neufchâteau area
3. Facilitate the capture of pillboxes and the advance by exerting pressure against the line of pillboxes along the border from the rear.
The German infantry were engaged by several Belgian patrols equipped with T-15 armoured cars. Several Belgian counterattacks were repulsed, among them an attack by the 1st Light Ardennes Infantry Division. Unsupported, the Germans faced a counterattack later in the evening by elements of the French 5th Cavalry Division, dispatched by General Charles Huntziger from the French 2nd Army, which had "massive" tank strength. The Germans were forced to retreat. The French, however, failed to pursue the fleeing German units, stopping at a dummy barrier. By the next morning, the 2nd Panzer Division had reached the area, and the mission had largely been accomplished. From the German perspective, the operation hindered rather than helped Heinz Guderian's Panzer Corps. The regiment had blocked the roads and against the odds, prevented French reinforcements reaching the Belgian–Franco-Luxembourg border, but it also destroyed Belgian telephone communications. This inadvertently prevented the Belgian field command recalling the units along the border. The 1st Belgian Light Infantry did not receive the signal to retreat and engaged in a severe fire-fight with the German armour, slowing down their advance.

The failure of the Franco–Belgian forces to hold the Ardennes gap was a fatal mistake. The Belgians had withdrawn laterally upon the initial invasion and had demolished and blocked routes of advance, which held up the French 2nd Army units moving north toward Namur and Huy. Devoid of any centre of resistance, the German assault engineers had cleared the obstacles unchallenged. The delay that the Belgian Ardennes Light Infantry, considered to be an elite formation, could have inflicted upon the advancing German armour was proved by the fight for Bodange where the 1st Panzer Division was held up for a total of eight hours. This battle was a result of a breakdown in communications and ran contrary to the operational intentions of the Belgian Army.

An abandoned Belgian Renault ACG1 tank, May 1940

Meanwhile, in the central Belgian sector, having failed to restore their front by means of ground attack, the Belgians attempted to bomb the bridges and positions that the Germans had captured intact and were holding on 11 May. An unspecified squadron which attempted to do so lost 11 out of 12 aircraft during one mission. The German counter-air operations were spearheaded by *Jagdgeschwader 26* under the command of Hans-Hugo Witt, which was responsible for 82 of the German claims in aerial combat between 11 and 13 May. Despite the apparent success of the German fighter units, the air battle was not one-sided. On the morning of 11 May, 10 Junkers Ju 87 *Stukas* of *Sturzkampfgeschwader 2* were shot down attacking Belgian forces in the Namur–Dinant gap, despite the presence of two other *Jagdgeschwader—27* and *51*. Nevertheless, the Germans reported a weakening in Allied air resistance in northern Belgium by 13 May.

During the night of 11 May, the British 3rd Infantry Division under the command of General Bernard Law Montgomery, reached its position on the Dyle river at Leuven. As it did so the Belgian 10th Infantry Division, occupying the position, mistook them for German parachutists and fired on them. The Belgians refused to yield but Montgomery claimed to have got his way by placing himself under the command of the Belgian forces, knowing that when the Germans came within artillery range the Belgians would withdraw.

Alan Brooke, commander of the British II Corps sought to put the matter of cooperation right with King Leopold. The King discussed the matter with Brooke, who felt a compromise could be reached. Van Overstraeten, the King's military aide, stepped in and said that the 10th Belgian Infantry Division could not be moved. Instead, the British should move further south and remain completely clear of Brussels. Brooke told the King that the 10th Belgian Division was on the wrong side of the Gamelin line and was exposed. Leopold deferred to his advisor and chief of staff. Brooke found Overstaeten to be ignorant of the situation and the dispositions of the B.E.F. Given that the left flank of the B.E.F rested on its Belgian ally, the British were now unsure about Belgian military capabilities. The Allies had more serious grounds for complaint about the Belgian anti-tank defences along the Dyle line, that covered the Namur–Perwez gap which was not protected by any natural obstacles. Only a few days before the attack, General Headquarters had discovered the Belgians had sited their anti-tank defences (*de Cointet* defences) several miles east of the Dyle between Namur–Perwez.

After holding onto the Albert Canal's west bank for nearly 36 hours, the 4th and 7th Belgian infantry divisions withdrew. The capture of Eben-Emael allowed the Germans to force through the Panzers of the 6th Army. The situation for the Belgian divisions was either to withdraw or be encircled. The Germans had advanced beyond Tongres and were now in a position to sweep south to Namur, which would threaten to envelope the entire Albert Canal and Liege positions. Under the circumstances, both divisions withdrew. On the evening of 11 May, the Belgian Command withdrew its forces behind the Namur–Antwerp line. The following day, the French 1st Army arrived at Gembloux, near Hannut, to cover the "Gembloux gap". It was a flat area, devoid of prepared or entrenched positions.

The French 7th Army, on the northern flank of the Belgian line, protected the Bruges–Ghent–Ostend axis and, covering the Channel ports, had advanced into Belgium and into the Netherlands with speed. It reached Breda in the Netherlands, on 11 May. But German parachute forces had seized the Moerdijk causeway on the Meuse river, splitting the Dutch state in two. The Dutch Army withdrew north to Rotterdam and Amsterdam, making it impossible for the French to link up. The French 7th Army continued east and met the 9th Panzer Division about 20 kilometres (12 mi) east of Breda at Tilburg. The battle resulted in the French retiring, in the face of *Luftwaffe* air assaults, to Antwerp. It would later help in the defence of the city. The *Luftwaffe* had given priority to attacking the French 7th Army's spearhead into the Netherlands as it threatened the Moerdijk bridgehead. *Kampfgeschwaders 40* and *54* supported by Ju 87s from *VIII. Fliegerkorps* helped drive them back. Fears of Allied reinforcements reaching Antwerp forced the *Luftwaffe* to cover the Scheldt estuary. *KG 30* bombed and sank two Dutch gunboats and three Dutch destroyers, as well as badly damaging two Royal Navy destroyers. But overall the bombing had a limited effect.

12–14 May: The battles of the central Belgian plain

During the night of 11/12 May, the Belgians were fully engaged in withdrawing to the Dyle line, covered by a network of demolitions and rearguards astride Tongres. During the morning of 12 May, King Leopold III, General van Overstraeten, Édouard Daladier, General Alphonse Georges (commander of the First Allied army Group, comprising the B.E.F, French 1st, 2nd, 7th and 9th Armies), General Gaston Billotte (coordinator of the Allied Armies) and General Henry Royds Pownall, Gort's chief of staff, met for a military conference near Mons. It was agreed the Belgian Army would man the Antwerp–Leuven line, while its allies took up the responsibility of defending the extreme north and south of the country. The Belgian III Corps, and its 1st Chasseurs Ardennais, 2nd Infantry and 3rd Infantry divisions had withdrawn from the Liege fortifications to avoid being encircled. One regiment, the Liege Fortress Regiment, stayed behind to disrupt German communications. Further to the south, the Namur fortress, manned by VI Corps' 5th Infantry Division and the 2nd Chasseurs Ardennais with the 12th French Infantry Division, fought delaying actions and participated in a lot of demolition work while guarding the position. As far as the Belgians were concerned, it had accomplished the only independent mission assigned to it: to hold the Liege–Albert Canal line long enough for the Allied units to reach friendly forces occupying the Namur–Antwerp–Givet line. For the remainder of the campaign, the Belgians would execute their operations in accordance with the overall Allied plan.

Belgian soldiers fought rearguard actions while other Belgian units already on the Dyle line worked tirelessly to organize better defensive positions in the Leuven–Antwerp gap. The 2nd Regiment of Guides and the 2nd Carabineers Cyclists of the 2nd Belgian Cavalry

Division covered the retreat of the 4th and 7th Belgian divisions and were particularly distinguished at the Battle of Tirlemont and the Battle of Haelen. In light of the withdrawal to the main defensive line, which was now being supported by the British and French Armies, King Leopold issued the following proclamation to improve morale after the defeats at the Albert Canal:
Soldiers

The Belgian Army, brutally assailed by an unparalleled surprise attack, grappling with forces that are better equipped and have the advantage of a formidable air force, has for three days carried out difficult operations, the success of which is of the utmost importance to the general conduct of the battle and to the result of war.

These operations require from all of us – officers and men – exceptional efforts, sustained day and night, despite a moral tension tested to its limits by the sight of the devastation wrought by a pitiless invader. However severe the trial may be, you will come through it gallantly.

Our position improves with every hour; our ranks are closing up. In the critical days that are ahead of us, you will summon up all your energies, you will make every sacrifice, to stem the invasion.

Just as they did in 1914 on the Yser, so now the French and British troops are counting on you: the safety and honour of the country are in your hands.
Leopold.

German tanks in western Belgium, May 1940

To the Allies, the Belgian failure to hold onto its eastern frontiers (they were thought to be capable of holding out for two weeks), was a disappointment. The Allied Chiefs of Staff had sought to avoid an encounter mobile battle without any strong fixed defences to fall back on and hoped Belgian resistance would last long enough for a defensive line to be established. Nevertheless, a brief lull fell on the Dyle front on 11 May which enabled the Allied armies to get into position by the time the first major assault was launched the following day. Allied cavalry had moved into position and infantry and artillery were reaching the front more slowly, by rail. Although unaware of it, the First Allied army Group and the Belgian Army outnumbered and outgunned Walther von Reichenau's German 6th Army.

On the morning of 12 May, in response to Belgian pressure and necessity, the Royal Air Force and the *Armée de l'Air* undertook several air attacks on the German-held Maastricht and Meuse bridges to prevent German forces flowing into Belgium. 74 sorties had been flown by the Allies since 10 May. On 12 May, 11 out of 18 French Breguet 693 bombers were shot down. The RAF Advanced Air Striking Force, which included the largest Allied bomber force, was reduced to 72 aircraft out of 135 by 12 May. For the next 24 hours missions were postponed as the German anti-aircraft and fighter defences were too strong.

The results of the bombing is difficult to determine. The German XIX Corps war diary's situation summary at 20:00 on 14 May noted:

The completion of the military bridge at Donchery had not yet been carried out owing to heavy flanking artillery fire and long bombing attacks on the bridging point ... Throughout the day all three divisions have had to endure constant air attack — especially at the crossing and bridging points. Our fighter cover is inadequate. Requests [for increased fighter protection] are still unsuccessful.

The *Luftwaffe's* operations includes a note of "vigorous enemy fighter activity through which our close reconnaissance in particular is severely impeded". Nevertheless, inadequate protection was given to cover RAF bombers against the strength of German opposition over the target area. In all, out of 109 Fairey Battles and Bristol Blenheims which had attacked enemy columns and communications in the Sedan area, 45 had been lost. On 15 May, daylight bombing was significantly reduced. Of 23 aircraft employed, four failed to return. Equally, owing to the Allied fighter presence, the German XIX Corps War Diary states, "Corps no longer has at its disposal its own long-range reconnaissance ... [Reconnaissance squadrons] are no longer in a position to carry out vigorous, extensive reconnaissance, as, owing to casualties, more than half of their aircraft are not now available."

General Erich Hoepner commanded XVI Army Corps at the Battle of Hannut and the Gembloux gap offensive

The most serious combat to evolve on 12 May 1940 was the beginning of the Battle of Hannut (12–14 May). While the German Army Group A advanced through the Belgian Ardennes, Army Group B's 6th Army launched an offensive operation toward the Gembloux gap. Gembloux occupied a position in the Belgian plain; it was an unfortified, untrenched space in the main Belgian defensive line. The Gap stretched from the southern end of the Dyle line, from Wavre in the north, to Namur in the south, 20 kilometres (12 mi) to 30 kilometres (19 mi). After attacking out of the Maastricht bulge and defeating the Belgian defences at Liege, which compelled the Belgian I Corps to retreat, the German 6th Army's XVI Panzer-Motorised Corps, under the command of General Erich Hoepner and containing the 3rd and 4th Panzer Divisions, launched an offensive in the area where the French mistakenly expected the main German thrust.

The Gembloux gap was defended by the French 1st Army, with six elite divisions including the 2nd (2e Division Légère Mécanique, or 2e DLM) and 3rd Light Mechanised Divisions. The Prioux Cavalry Corps, under the command of Rene-Jacques-Adolphe Prioux, was to advance 30 kilometres (19 mi) beyond the line (east) to provide a screen for the move. The French 1st and 2nd Armoured Divisions were to be moved behind the French 1st Army to defend its main lines in depth. The Prioux Cavalry Corps was equal to a German Panzer Corps and was to occupy a screening line on the Tirlemont–Hannut–Huy axis. The operational plan called for the Corps to delay the German advance on Gembloux and Hannut until the main elements of the French 1st Army had reached Gembloux and dug in.

Hoepner's Panzer Corps and Prioux' Cavalry clashed head-on near Hannut, Belgium, on 12 May. Contrary to popular belief, the Germans did not outnumber the French. Frequently, figures of 623 German and 415 French tanks are given. The German 3rd and 4th Panzer Divisions numbered 280 and 343 respectively. The 2e DLM and 3e DLM numbered 176 Somuas and 239 Hotchkiss H35s. Added to this force were the considerable number of Renault AMR-ZT-63s in the Cavalry Corps. The R35 was equal or superior to the Panzer I and Panzer IIs in armament terms. This applies all the more to the 90 Panhard 178 armoured cars of the French Army. Its 25mm main gun could penetrate the armour of the Panzer IV. In terms of tanks that were capable of engaging and surviving a tank-vs-tank action, the Germans possessed just 73 Panzer IIIs and 52 Panzer IVs. The French had 176 SOMUA and 239 Hotchkisses. German tank units also contained 486 Panzer I and IIs, which were of dubious combat value given their losses in the Polish Campaign.

The German forces were able to communicate by radio during the battle and they could shift the point of the main effort unexpectedly. The Germans also practised combined arms tactics, while the French tactical deployment was a rigid and linear leftover from the First World War. French tanks did not possess radios and often the commanders had to dismount to issue orders. Despite the disadvantages experienced by the Germans in armour, they were able to gain the upper hand in the morning battle on 12 May, encircling several French battalions. The combat power of the French 2e DLM managed to defeat the German defences guarding the pockets and freeing the trapped units. Contrary to German reports, the French were victorious on that first day, preventing a Wehrmacht break-through to Gembloux or seizing Hannut. The result of the first day's battle was:

The effect on the German light tanks was catastrophic. Virtually every French weapon from 25mm upward penetrated the 7-13mm of the Panzer I. Although the Panzer II fared somewhat better, especially those that had been uparmoured since the Polish Campaign, their losses were high. Such was the sheer frustration of the crews of these light Panzers in [the] face of heavier armoured French machines that some resorted to desperate expedients. One account speaks of a German Panzer commander attempting to climb on a Hotchkiss H-35 with a hammer, presumably to smash the machine's periscopes, but falling off and being crushed by the tank's tracks. Certainly by day's end, Prioux had reason to claim that his tanks had come off best. The battlefield around Hannut was littered with knocked-out tanks–the bulk of which were German Panzers–with by far and away the bulk of them being Panzer Is and IIs.

The following day, 13 May, the French were undone by their poor tactical deployment. They strung their armour out in a thin line between Hannut and Huy, leaving no defence in depth, which was the point of sending the French armour to the Gembloux gap in the first place. This left Hoepner with a chance to mass against one of the French Light Divisions (the 3e DLM) and achieve a breakthrough in that sector. Moreover, with no reserves behind the front, the French denied themselves the chance of a counterattack. The victory saw the Panzer Corps out-manoeuvre the 2e DLM on its left flank. The Belgian III Corps, retreating from Liege, offered to support the French front held by the 3e DLM. This offer was rejected.

On 12 and 13 May, 2e DLM lost no AFVs, but the 3e DLM lost 30 SOMUAs and 75 Hotchkisses. The French had disabled 160 German tanks. But as the poor linear deployment had allowed the Germans the chance of breaking through in one spot, the entire battlefield had to be abandoned, the Germans repaired nearly three quarters of their tanks; 49 were destroyed and 111 were repaired. They had 60 men killed and another 80 wounded. In terms of battlefield casualties, the Hannut battle had resulted in the French knocking-out 160 German tanks, losing 105 themselves. Prioux had achieved his tactical mission and withdrew.

Hoepner now pursued the retreating French. Being impatient, he did not wait for his infantry divisions to catch up. Instead, he hoped to continue pushing the French back and not give them time to construct a coherent defence line. German formations pursued the enemy to Gembloux. The Panzer Corps ran into retreating French columns and inflicted heavy losses on them. The pursuit created severe problems for the French artillery. The combat was so closely fought that the danger of friendly fire incidents were very real. Nevertheless the French, setting up new anti-tank screens and Hoepner, lacking infantry support, caused the Germans to attack positions head-on. During the following Battle of Gembloux the two Panzer Divisions reported heavy losses during 14 May and were forced to slow their pursuit. The German attempts to capture Gembloux were repulsed.

Although suffering numerous tactical reverses, operationally the Germans diverted the Allied First Army Group from the lower Ardennes area. In the process his forces, along with the *Luftwaffe* depleted Prioux' Cavalry Corps. When news of the German breakthrough at Sedan reached Prioux, he withdrew from Gembloux. With the Gembloux gap breached, the German Panzer Corps, the 3rd and 4th Panzer Divisions, were no longer required by Army Group B and were handed over to Army Group A. Army Group B would continue its own offensive to force the collapse of the Meuse front. The Army Group was in a position to advance westward to Mons, outflank the B.E.F and Belgian Army protecting the Dyle–Brussels sector, or turn south to outflank the French 9th Army. German losses had been heavy at Hannut and Gembloux. The 4th Panzer Division was down to 137 tanks on 16 May, including just four Panzer IVs. The 3rd Panzer Division was down by 20–25 percent of its operational force, while the 4th Panzer Division 45–50 percent of its tanks were not combat ready. Damaged tanks were quickly repaired, but its strength was initially greatly weakened. The French 1st Army had also taken a battering and despite winning several tactical defensive victories it was forced to retreat on 15 May owing to developments elsewhere, leaving its tanks on the battlefield, while the Germans were free to recover theirs.

15–21 May: Counterattacks and retreat to the coast

German infantry in western Belgium in May, 1940.

On the morning of 15 May, German Army Group A broke the defences at Sedan and was now free to drive for the English Channel. The Allies considered a wholesale withdrawal from the Belgian trap. The withdrawal would reflect three stages: the night of 16/17 May to the River Senne, the night of 17/18 May to the river Dendre and the night of 18/19 May to the river Scheldt. The Belgians were reluctant to abandon Brussels and Leuven, especially as the Dyle line had withstood German pressure well. The Belgian Army, the B.E.F and the French 1st Army, in a domino effect, was ordered/forced to retire on 16 May to avoid their southern flanks from being turned by the German armoured forces advancing through the French Ardennes and the German 6th Army advancing through Gembloux. The Belgian Army was holding the German Fourteenth Army on the K.W line, along with the French 7th and British armies. Had it not been for the collapse of the French 2nd Army at Sedan, the Belgians were confident that they could have checked the German advance.

The situation called for the French and British to abandon the Antwerp–Namur line and strong positions in favour of improvised positions behind the Scheldt, without facing any real resistance. In the South, General Deffontaine of the Belgian VII Corps retreated from the Namur and Liege regions, the Liege fortress region put up stiff resistance to the German 6th Army. In the North, the 7th Army was diverted to Antwerp after the surrender of the Dutch on 15 May, but was then diverted to support the French 1st Army. In the centre, the Belgian Army and the B.E.F suffered little German pressure. On 15 May, the only sector to really be tested was around Leuven, which was held by the British 3rd Division. Thereafter the B.E.F was not pursued vigorously to the Scheldt.

After the withdrawal of the French Army from the northern sector, the Belgians were left to guard the fortified city of Antwerp. Four infantry divisions (including the 13th and 17th Reserve Infantry Divisions) engaged the German Eighteenth Army's 208th, 225th and 526th Infantry Divisions. The Belgians successfully defended the northern part of the city, delaying the German infantry forces while starting to withdraw from Antwerp on 16 May. The city fell on 18/19 May after considerable Belgian resistance. On 18 May the Belgians received word that Namur's Fort Marchovelette had fallen; Suarlee fell on 19 May; St. Heribert and Malonne on 21 May; Dave, Maizeret and Andoy on 23 May.

Between 16 and 17 May, the British and French withdrew behind the Willebroek Canal, as the volume of Allied forces in Belgium fell and moved toward the German armoured thrust from the Ardennes. The Belgian I Corps and V Corps also retreated to what the Belgians called the Ghent bridgehead, behind the Dendre and Scheldt. The Belgian Artillery Corps and its infantry support defeated attacks by the Eighteenth Army's infantry and in a communiqué from London, the British recognised the "Belgian Army has contributed largely towards the success of the defensive battle now being fought. Nevertheless, the now-outnumbered Belgians abandoned Brussels and the Government fled to Ostend. The city was occupied by the German Army on 17 May. The very next morning, Hoepner, the German XVI Corps commander, was ordered to release the 3rd and 4th Panzer Divisions to Army Group A. This left the 9th Panzer Division attached to the Eighteenth Army as the only armoured unit on the Belgian front.

By 19 May, the Germans were hours away from reaching the French Channel coast. Gort had discovered the French had neither plan nor reserves and little hope for stopping the German thrust to the channel. He was concerned that the French 1st Army on its southern flank had been reduced to a disorganised mass of "fag-ends", fearing that German armour might appear on their right flank at Arras or Péronne, striking for the channel ports at Calais or Boulogne or north west into the British flank. Their position in Belgium massively compromised, the B.E.F. considered abandoning Belgium and retreating to Ostend,

Bruges or Dunkirk, the latter lying some 10 kilometres (6.2 mi) to 15 kilometres (9.3 mi) inside the French border.

A Belgian Renault ACG1 tank, knocked out during the Battle for Antwerp, 19 May 1940

The proposals of a British strategic withdrawal from the continent was rejected by the War Cabinet and the Chief of the Imperial General Staff (CIGS). They dispatched General Ironside to inform Gort of their decision and to order him to conduct an offensive to the south-west "through all opposition" to reach the "main French forces" in the south [the strongest French forces were actually in the north]. The Belgian Army was asked to conform to the plan, or should they choose, the British Royal Navy would evacuate what units they could. The British cabinet decided that even if the "Somme offensive" was carried out successfully, some units may still need to be evacuated, and ordered Admiral Ramsay to assemble a large number of vessels. This was the beginning of Operation Dynamo. Ironside arrived at British General Headquarters at 06:00 am on 20 May, the same day that continental communications between the France and Belgium were cut. When Ironside made his proposals known to Gort, Gort replied such an attack was impossible. Seven of his nine divisions were engaged on the Scheldt and even if it was possible to withdraw them, it would create a gap between the Belgians and British which the enemy could exploit and encircle the former. The B.E.F had been marching and fighting for nine days and was now running short of ammunition. The main effort had to be made by the French to the south.

The Belgian position on any offensive move was made clear by King Leopold III. As far as he was concerned, the Belgian Army could not conduct offensive operations as it lacked tanks and aircraft; it existed solely for defence. The King also made clear that in the rapidly shrinking area of Belgium still free, there was only enough food for two weeks. Leopold did not expect the B.E.F to jeopardize its own position in order to keep contact with the Belgian Army, but he warned the British that if it persisted with the southern offensive the Belgians would be overstretched and their army would collapse. King Leopold suggested the best recourse was to establish a beach-head covering Dunkirk and the Belgian channel ports. The will of the CIGS won out. Gort committed just two infantry battalions and the only armoured battalion in the B.E.F to the attack, which despite some initial tactical success, failed to break the German defensive line at the Battle of Arras on 21 May.

In the aftermath of this failure, the Belgians were asked to fall back to the Yser river and protect the Allied left flank and rear areas. The King's aide, General Overstraten said that such a move could not be made and would lead to the Belgian Army disintegrating. Another plan for further offensives was suggested. The French requested the Belgians withdraw to the Leie and the British to the French frontier between Maulde and Halluin, the Belgians were then to extend their front to free further parts of the B.E.F for the attack. The French 1st Army would relieve two more divisions on the right flank. Leopold was reluctant to undertake such a move because it would abandon all but a small portion of Belgium. The Belgian Army was exhausted and it was an enormous technical task that would take too long to complete.

At this time, the Belgians and the British concluded that the French were beaten and the Allied Armies in the pocket on the Belgian–Franco border would be destroyed if action was not taken. The British, having lost confidence in their Allies, decided to look to the survival of the B.E.F.

22–28 May: Last defensive battles

The Germans advance to the English Channel.

The Belgian battle-front on the morning of 22 May extended some 90 kilometres (56 mi). From north to south, beginning with the Cavalry Corps which checked its advance at Terneuzen. V, II, VI, VII and IV Corps (all Belgian), were drawn up side by side. Two further signal Corps were guarding the coast. These formations were now largely holding the eastern front as the B.E.F and French forces withdrew to the west to protect Dunkirk, which was vulnerable to German assault on 22 May. The eastern front remained intact, but the Belgians now occupied its last fortified position at Leie. The Belgian I Corps, with only two incomplete divisions, had been heavily engaged in the fighting and the their line was wearing thin. On that day, Winston Churchill visited the front and pressed for the French and British Armies to break-out from the north-east. He assumed that the Belgian Cavalry Corps could support the offensives' right flank. Churchill dispatched the following message to Gort:

1. That the Belgian Army should withdraw to the line of the Yser and stand there, the sluices being opened.
2. That the British Army and French 1st Army should attack south-west towards Bapaume and Cambrai at the earliest moment, certainly tomorrow, with about eight divisions, and with the Bel-

gian Cavalry Corps on the right of the British.

Such an order ignored the fact that the Belgian Army could not withdraw to the Yser, and there was little chance of any Belgian Cavalry joining in the attack. The plan for the Belgian withdrawal was sound, the Yser river covered Dunkirk to the east and south, while the La Bassée Canal covered it from the west. The ring of the Yser also dramatically shorted the Belgian Army's area of operations. Such a move would have abandoned Passchendaele and Ypres and would have certainly meant the capture of Ostend while further reducing the amount of Belgian territory still free by a few square miles. And of course it would have meanth the loss of all Belgian ports to the East of the Yser, like Zeebrugge and Ostend.

On 23 May, the French tried to conduct a series of offensives against the German defensive line on the Ardennes–Calais axis but failed to make any meaningful gains. Meanwhile, on the Belgian front, the Belgians, under pressure, retreated further, and the Germans captured Terneuzen and Ghent that day. The Belgians also had trouble moving the oil, food and ammunition that they had left. The *Luftwaffe* had air superiority and made everyday life hazardous in logistical terms. Air support could only be called in by "wireless" and the RAF was operating from bases in southern England which made communication more difficult. The French denied the use of the Dunkirk, Bourbourg and Gravelines bases to the Belgians, which had initially been placed at its disposal. The Belgians were forced to use the only harbours left to them, at Nieuport and Ostend.

Churchill and Maxime Weygand, who had taken over command from Gamelin, were still determined to break the German line and extricate their forces to the south. When they communicated their intentions to King Leopold and van Overstraten on 24 May, the latter was stunned. A dangerous gap was starting to open between the British and Belgians between Ypres and Menen, which threatened what remained of the Belgian front. The Belgians could not cover it, such a move would have overstretched them. Without consulting the French or asking permission from his government, Gort immediately and decisively ordered the British 5th and 50th Infantry Divisions to plug the gap and abandon any offensive operations further south.

On the afternoon of 24 May, Von Bock had thrown four divisions, of Reichenau's 6th Army, against the Belgian IV Corps position at the Kortrijk area of the Leie. The Germans managed, against fierce resistance, to cross the river at night and force a one mile penetration along a 13-mile front between Wijik and Kortrijk. The Germans, with superior numbers and in command of the air, had won the bridgehead. Nevertheless, the Belgians had inflicted many casualties and several tactical defeats on the Germans. The 1st, 3rd, 9th and 10th Infantry Divisions, acting as reinforcements, had counterattacked several times and managed to capture 200 German prisoners. Belgian artillery and infantry were then heavily attacked by the *Luftwaffe* which forced their defeat. The Belgians blamed the French and British for not providing air cover. The German bridgehead dangerously exposed the eastern flank of the southward stretched B.E.F's 4th Infantry Division. Montgomery dispatched several units of the 3rd Infantry Division (including the heavy infantry of the 1st and 7th Middlesex battalions and the 99th Battery, 20th Anti-Tank Regiment), as an improvised defence.

A critical point of the "Weygand Plan" and the British Government and French Army's argument for a thrust south, was the withdrawal of forces to see the offensive through which had left the Belgian Army over-extended and was instrumental in its collapse. It was forced to cover the areas held by the B.E.F in order to enable the latter to engage in the offensive. Such a collapse could have resulted in the loss of the Channel ports behind the Allied front, leading to a complete strategic encirclement. The B.E.F could have done more to counterattack von Bock's left flank to relieve the Belgians as von Bock attacked *across* the fortified British position at Kortrijk. The Belgian High Command made at least five appeals for the British to attack the vulnerable left flank of the German divisions between the Scheldt and the Leie to avert disaster.

Admiral Sir Roger Keyes transmitted the following message to GHQ:
Van Overstraten is desperately keen for strong British counterattack. Either north or south of Leie could help restore the situation. Belgians expect to be attacked on the Ghent front tomorrow. Germans already have a bridgehead over canal west of Eecloo. There can be no question of the Belgian withdrawal to Yser. One battalion on march NE of Ypres was practically wiped out today in attack by sixty aircraft. Withdrawal over open roads without adequate fighter support very costly. Whole of their supplies are east of Yser. They strongly represent attempt should be made to restore the situation on Leie by British counter-attack for which opportunity may last another few hours only.
No such attack came. The Germans brought fresh reserves to cover the gap (Menen–Ypres). This nearly cut the Belgians off from the British. The 2nd, 6th and 10th Cavalry Divisions frustrated German attempts to exploit the gap in depth but the situation was still critical. On 26 May, Operation Dynamo officially commenced, in which large French and British contingents were to be evacuated to the United Kingdom. By that time the Royal Navy had already withdrawn 28,000 British non-fighting troops. Boulogne had fallen and Calais was about to, leaving Dunkirk, Ostend and Zeebrugge as the only viable ports which could be used for evacuation. The advance of the 14th German Army would not leave Ostend available for much longer. To the west, the German Army Group A had reached Dunkirk and were 4 miles (6.4 km) from its centre on the morning of 27 May, bringing the port within artillery range.

The situation on 27 May had changed considerably from just 24 hours earlier.

The Belgian Army had been forced from the Leie line on 26 May, and Nevele, Vynckt, Thelt and Iseghem had fallen on the western and central part of the Leie front. In the east the Germans had reached the outskirts of Bruges, and captured Ursel. In the west, the Menen–Ypres line had broken at Kortrijk and the Belgians were now using railway trucks to help form anti-tank defences on a line from Ypres–Passchendaele–Roulers. Further to the west the B.E.F had been forced back, north of Lille just over the French border and was now in danger of allowing a gap to develop between themselves and the Belgian southern flank on the Ypres–Lille axis. The danger in allowing a German advance to Dunkirk would mean the loss of the port which was now too great. The British withdrew to the port on 26 May. In doing so they left the French 1st Army's northeastern flank near Lille exposed. As the British moved out the Germans moved in, encircling the bulk of the French Army. Both Gort and his Chief of Staff, General Henry Pownall accepted that their withdrawal would mean the destruction of the French 1st Army, and they would be blamed for it.

The fighting of 26–27 May had brought the Belgian Army to the brink of collapse. The Belgians still held the Ypres–Roulers line to the west, and the Bruges–Thelt line to the east. However, on 27 May the central front collapsed in the Iseghem–Thelt sector. There was now nothing to prevent a German thrust to the east to take Ostend and Bruges, or west to take the ports at Nieuport or La Panne, deep in the Allied rear. The Belgians had practically exhausted all available means of resistance. The disintegration of the Belgian Army and its front caused many erroneous accusations by the British. In fact, on numerous occasions, the Belgians had held on after British withdrawals. One example was the taking over of the Scheldt line, where they relieved the British 44th Infantry Division, allowing it to retire through their ranks. Despite this, Gort and to a greater extent Pownall, showed unjust contempt for the Belgians. When it was enquired if any Belgians were to be evacuated, Pownall was reported to have replied, "We don't care a bugger what happens to the Belgians".

Belgian surrender

The Belgian Army was stretched from Cadzand south to Menin on the river Leie, and west, from Menin, to Bruges without any sort of reserves. With the exception of a few RAF sorties, the air was exclusively under the control of the *Luftwaffe*, and the Belgians reported attacks against all targets considered an objective, with resulting casualties. No natural obstacles remained between the Belgians and the German Army, retreat was not feasible. The *Luftwaffe* had destroyed most of the rail networks to Dunkirk, just three roads were left: Bruges–Thourout–Dixmude, Bruges–Ghistelles–Nieuport and Bruges–Ostende–Nieuport. Using such axes of retreat was impossible without losses owing to German air supremacy (as opposed to air superiority). Water supplies were damaged and cut off, gas and electricity supplies were also cut. Canals were drained and used as supply dumps for whatever ammunition and food-stuffs were left. The total remaining area covered just 1,700 km², and compacted military and civilians alike, of which the latter numbered some 3 million people. Under these circumstances Leopold deemed further resistance useless. On the evening of 27 May, he requested an armistice.

Churchill sent a message to Keyes the same day, and made clear what he thought of the request:
Belgian Embassy here assumes from King's decision to remain that he regards the war as lost and contemplates [a] separate peace. It is in order to dissociate itself from this that the constitutional Belgian Government has reassembled on foreign soil. Even if present Belgian Army has to lay down its arms, there are 200,000 Belgians of military age in France, and greater resources than Belgium had in 1914 which to fight back. By present decision the King is dividing the Nation and delivering it into Hitler's protection. Please convey these considerations to the King, and impress upon him the disastrous consequences to the Allies and to Belgium of his present choice.

Negotiating the Belgian capitulation

The Royal Navy evacuated General Headquarters at Middelkerke and St. Andrews, east of Bruges, during the night. Leopold III, and his mother Queen Mother Elisabeth, stayed in Belgium to endure five years of self-imposed captivity. In response to the advice of his government to set up a government-in-exile Leopold said, "I have decided to stay. The cause of the Allies is lost." The Belgian surrender came into effect at 04:00 on 28 May. Recriminations abounded with the British and French claiming the Belgians had betrayed the alliance. In Paris, the French Premier Paul Reynaud, denounced Leopold's surrender, the Belgian Premier Hubert Pierlot, informed the people that Leopold had taken action against the unanimous advice of the government. As a result, the king was no longer in a position to govern and the Belgian government-in-exile that was located in Paris (later moved to London following the fall of France), would continue the struggle. The chief complaint was that the Belgians had not given any prior warning that their situation was so serious as to capitulate. Such claims were largely unjust. The Allies had known, and admitted it privately on 25 May through contact with the Belgians, that the latter were on the verge of collapse. Churchill's and the British response was officially restrained. This was due to the strong-willed defence of the Belgian defensive campaign presented to the cabinet by Sir Roger Keyes at 11:30 am 28 May. The French and Belgian ministers had referred to

Leopold's actions as treacherous, but they were unaware of the true events: Leopold had not signed an agreement with Hitler in order to form a collaborative government, but an unconditional surrender as Commander-in-Chief of the Belgian Armed Forces.

Casualties

The casualty reports include total losses at this point in the campaign. The figures for the Battle of Belgium, 10–28 May 1940, cannot be known with any certainty.

Belgian casualties

Belgian casualties stood at:
- Killed in action: 6,093 and 2,000 prisoners of war died in captivity
- Missing: more than 500
- Captured: 200,000
- Wounded: 15,850
- Aircraft: 112 destroyed

French casualties

Numbers for the Battle of Belgium are unknown, but the French suffered the following losses throughout the entire western campaign, 10 May – 22 June:
- Killed in action: 90,000
- Wounded: 200,000
- Prisoners of War: 1.9.
- Total French losses in aircraft numbered 264 from 12 to 25 May, and 50 for 26 May to 1 June.

British casualties

Numbers for the Battle of Belgium are unknown, but the British suffered the following losses throughout the entire campaign, 10 May – 22 June:
- 68,111 killed in action, wounded or captured.
- 64,000 vehicles destroyed or abandoned
- 2,472 guns destroyed or abandoned
- RAF losses throughout the entire campaign (10 May – 22 June) amounted to 931 aircraft and 1,526 casualties. Casualties to 28 May are unknown. Total British losses in the air numbered 344 between 12 and 25 May, and 138 between 26 May and 1 June.

German casualties

The consolidated report of the *Oberkommando der Wehrmacht* regarding the operations in the west from 10 May to 4 June (German: *Zusammenfassender Bericht des Oberkommandos der Wehrmacht über die Operationen im Westen vom 10. Mai bis 4. Juni*) reports:
- Killed in action: 10,232 officers and soldiers
- Missing: 8,463 officers and soldiers
- Wounded: 42,523 officers and soldiers
- Losses of the Luftwaffe from 10 May to 3 June: 432 aircraft
- Losses of the Kriegsmarine: none

Source (edited): "http://en.wikipedia.org/wiki/Battle_of_Belgium"

Battle of Belgium (1940) order of battle

This is the order of battle for the Battle of Belgium, a World War II battle between German and Western Allies in Belgium between 10–28 May 1940.

Allied armed forces

Belgian air service (Aéronautique Militaire Belge)

The Belgian air service comprised three main aerial regiments:
- 1er Régiment d'Aéronautique (1st Air Regiment - Observation and Army Cooperation aircraft)
- 2e Régiment d'Aéronautique (2nd Air Regiment - Equipped with Fighter aircraft)
- 3e Régiment d'Aéronautique (3rd Air Regiment - Reconnaissance and Bombers aircraft)

The Aéronautique Militaire Belge was reinforced by the Royal Air Force:
- RAF Advanced Air Striking Force (Air Vice-Marshal P H L Playfair)
- No. 14 Group RAF (Group Captain P.F. Fullard)

Belgian Army

The strength of the Belgian Army extended to seven Corps:
- - **Belgian I Corps**
    - 1st Infantry Division
    - 4th Infantry Division
    - 7th Infantry Division
  - **Belgian II Corps**
    - 6th Infantry Division
    - 11th Infantry Division
    - 14th Infantry Division
  - **Belgian III Corps**
    - 1st Chasseurs Ardennais
    - 2nd Infantry Division
    - 3rd Infantry Division
  - **Belgian IV Corps**
    - 9th Infantry Division
    - 15th Infantry Division
    - 18th Infantry Division
  - **Belgian V Corps**
    - 12th Infantry Division
    - 13th Infantry Division
    - 17th Infantry Division
  - **Belgian VI Corps**
    - 5th Infantry Division
    - 10th Infantry Division
    - 16th Infantry Division
  - **Belgian VII Corps**
    - 8th Infantry Division
    - 1st Chasseurs Ardennais
  - **Belgian Cavalry Corps**
    - 1st Cavalry Division
    - 2nd Cavalry Division

French First Army Group

French 1st Army

- **French Cavalry Corps**
  - 2nd Light Mechanized Division
  - 3rd Light Mechanized Division
- **French 3rd Corps**
  - 1st Moroccan Infantry Division
  - 2nd North African Infantry Division
- **French 4th Corps**
  - 32nd Infantry Division
- **French 5th Corps**
  - 5th North African Infantry Division
  - 101st Infantry Division
- **Belgian VII Corps**
  - 2nd Chasseurs Ardennais

- 8th Infantry Division

French 2nd Army

- *Direct reporting:*
  - 2nd Light Cavalry Division
  - 5th Light Cavalry Division
  - 1st Cavalry Brigade
- **French 10th Corps**
  - 3rd North African Infantry Division
  - 5th Light Cavalry Division
  - 55th Infantry Division
  - 71st Infantry Division
- **French 18th Corps**
  - 1st Colonial Infantry Division
  - 41st Infantry Division

French 7th Army

- *Direct reporting:*
  - 21st Infantry Division
  - 60th Infantry Division
  - 68th Infantry Division
- **French 1st Corps**
  - 1st Light Mechanized Division
  - 25th Motorized Division
- **French 16th Corps**
  - 9th Motorized Division

French 9th Army

- *Direct reporting:*
  - 4th North African Infantry Division
  - 53rd Infantry Division
- **French 2nd Corps**
  - 4th Light Cavalry Division
  - 5th Motorized Division
- **French 11th Corps**
  - 1st Light Cavalry Division
  - 18th Infantry Division
  - 22nd Infantry Division
- **French 41st Corps**
  - 61st Infantry Division
  - 102nd Fortress Division
  - 3rd Spahi Brigade

British Expeditionary Force

General **Lord Gort**

- *Directly reporting:*
  - 5th Infantry Division
  - 12th Infantry Division
  - 23rd Infantry Division
  - 46th Infantry Division
- **British I Corps** - Lieutenant-General **Michael Barker**
  - 1st Infantry Division
  - 2nd Infantry Division
  - 48th Infantry Division
- **British II Corps** - Lieutenant-General **Alan Brooke**
  - 3rd Infantry Division
  - 4th Infantry Division
  - 50th Infantry Division
- **British III Corps** - Lieutenant-General **Ronald Adam**
  - 42nd Infantry Division
  - 44th Infantry Division

German armed forces

German Army Group B

Commanded by Colonel General **Fedor von Bock**

- (Chief of Staff - Lt.Gen. Hans von Salmuth).
- **German Sixth Army** —Colonel General **Walter von Reichenau**
  - (Chief of Staff - Maj.Gen. Friedrich Paulus).
  - IV Corps - Gen.of Infantry Viktor von Schwedler
    - 15th Infantry Division - Maj.Gen. Ernst-Eberhard Hell (reserve)
    - 205th Infantry Division - Lt.Gen. Ernst Richter
  - XI Corps- Lt.Gen. Joachim von Kortzfleisch
    - 7th Infantry Division - Maj.Gen. Eccard von Gablenz
    - 211th Infantry Division - Maj.Gen. Kurt Renner
    - 253rd Infantry Division - Lt.Gen. Fritz Kuhne
  - IX Corps
  - XVI Corps
    - 3rd Panzer Division
    - 4th Panzer Division
  - XXVII Corps
- German Eighteenth Army — Georg von Küchler
  - Reserves
    - 208th Infantry Division
    - 225th Infantry Division
    - 526th Infantry Division
  - SS "Verfügungstruppe" Division
  - 7th Airborne Division
  - 22nd Air Landing Infantry Division
  - 9th Panzer Division
  - 207th Infantry Division
  - X Corps
    - SS "Adolf Hitler" Division
    - 227th Infantry Division
    - 1st Cavalry Division
  - XXVI Corps
    - 256th Infantry Division
    - 254th Infantry Division
    - SS "Der Führer" Division

Luftwaffe

The Luftwaffe order of battle for operations over Belgium:

- IV. **Fliegerkorps** (General der Flieger, Generaloberst Alfred Keller)
  - *Lehrgeschwader 1* (Stab. I., II., III., IV. Düsseldorf)
  - *Kampfgeschwader 30* (Stab. I., II., at Oldenburg III. at Marx)
  - *Kampfgeschwader 27* (III. at Wunstorf)
- *Jagdfliegerführer 2* (*Oberst* Kurt-Bertram von Döring)
  - *Jagdgeschwader 26* (Stab., II at Dortmund, III. at (Essen-Mühlheim).)
  - *Jagdgeschwader 3* (III. at Hopsten)
  - *Jagdgeschwader 51* (Stab. at Bönninghardt, I. at Krefeld)
  - *Jagdgeschwader 27* (II. Bönninghardt)
  - *Jagdgeschwader 20* (I. at Bönninghardt)
- VIII. **Fliegerkorps** (Generalmajor Wolfram von Richthofen)
  - *Jagdgeschwader 27* (Stab.,I.)
  - *Jagdgeschwader 21*
  - *Jagdgeschwader 1* (I.)
  - *Sturzkampfgeschwader 76* (I.)
  - *Sturzkampfgeschwader 2* (Stab., I., III.)
  - *Sturzkampfgeschwader 77* (Stab., I., II.)
  - *Lehrgeschwader 1* (IV(St.))
  - *Lehrgeschwader 2* II.(Shl)
  - *Kampfgeschwader 77* (Stab., I., II., III.)

Source (edited): "http://en.wikipedia.org/wiki/Battle_of_Belgium_(1940)_order_of_battle"

Battle of Fort Eben-Emael

The **Battle of Fort Eben-Emael** was a battle between Belgian and German forces that took place between 10 May and 11 May 1940, and was part of the Battle of the Netherlands, Battle of Belgium and Fall Gelb, the German invasion of the Low Countries and France. An assault force of German *Fallschirmjäger* were tasked with assaulting and capturing Fort Eben-Emael, a Belgian fortress whose artillery pieces dominated several important bridges over the Albert Canal which German forces intended to use to advance into Belgium. As some of the German airborne troops assaulted the fortress and disabled the garrison and the artillery pieces inside it, others simultaneously captured three bridges over the Canal. Having disabled the fortress, the airborne troops were then ordered to protect the bridges against Belgian counter-attacks until they linked up with ground forces from the German 18th Army.

The battle was a decisive victory for the German forces, with the airborne troops landing on top of the fortress via the use of gliders and using explosives and flamethrowers to disable the outer defences of the fortress. The *Fallschirmjäger* then entered the fortress, killing a number of defenders and containing the rest in the lower sections of the fortress. Simultaneously, the rest of the German assault force had landed near the three bridges over the Canal, destroyed a number of pillboxes and defensive positions and defeated the Belgian forces guarding the bridges, capturing them and bringing them under German control. The airborne troops suffered heavy casualties during the operation, but succeeded in holding the bridges until the arrival of German ground forces, who then aided the airborne troops in assaulting the fortress a second time and forcing the surrender of the remaining members of the garrison. German forces were then able to utilize two bridges over the Canal to bypass a number of Belgian defensive positions and advance into Belgium to aid in the invasion of the country. The bridge at Kanne was destroyed.

Background

On 10 May 1940 Germany launched Fall Gelb, an invasion of the Low Countries. By attacking through the Netherlands, Luxembourg and Belgium, the German Oberkommando der Wehrmacht believed that German forces could outflank the Maginot Line and then advance through southern Belgium and into northern France, cutting off the British Expeditionary Force and a large number of French forces and forcing the French government to surrender. To gain access to northern France, German forces would have to defeat the armed forces of the Low Countries and either bypass or neutralize a number of defensive positions, primarily in Belgium and the Netherlands. Some of these defensive positions were only lightly defended and intended more as delaying positions than true defensive lines designed to stop an enemy attack. However, a number of them were of a more permanent design, possessing considerable fortifications and garrisoned by significant numbers of troops. The Grebbe-Peel Line in the Netherlands, which stretched from the southern shore of the Zuider Zee to the Belgian border near Weert, had a large number of fortifications combined with natural obstacles, such as marsh-lands and the Geld Valley, which could easily be flooded to impede an attack. The Belgian defences consisted of one delaying position running along the Albert Canal, and then a main defensive line running along the River Dyle, which protected the port of Antwerp and the Belgian capital, Brussels. This delaying position was protected by a number of forward positions manned by troops, except in a single area where the canal ran close to the Dutch border, which was known as the 'Maastricht Appendix' due to the proximity of the city of Maastricht. The Belgian military could not build forward positions due to the proximity of the border, and therefore assigned an infantry division to guard the three bridges over the canal in the area, a brigade being assigned to each bridge. The bridges were defended by blockhouses equipped with machine-guns, and artillery support was provided by Fort Eben Emael, whose artillery pieces covered each of the two bridges. Having become aware of the Belgian defensive plan, which called for Belgian forces to briefly hold the delaying positions along the Albert Canal and then retreat to link up with British and French forces at the main defensive positions on the River Dyle, the German High Command made its own plans to disrupt this and seize and secure these three bridges, as well as a number of other bridges in Belgium and the Netherlands, to allow their own forces to breach the defensive positions and advance into the Netherlands.

Prelude

Belgian Preparation

The Belgian 7th Infantry Division was assigned to guard the three bridges over the canal, supplementing the troops who garrisoned Fort Eben Emael at the time of the battle. The bridge defences consisted of four large concrete pillboxes on the western side of the canal per bridge, three equipped with machine-guns and a fourth with an anti-tank gun; the bunker containing the anti-tank gun was positioned close to the road leading from the bridge, with one machine-gun equipped bunker immediately behind the bridge and two others flanking the bridge a short distance either side. A company position existed on the western bank of the canal by each of the bridges, with a small observation post on the eastern side which could be quickly recalled, and all three bridges could be destroyed with demolition charges set into their structures, triggered by a firing mechanism situated in the anti-tank bunkers. Fort Eben Emael, which measured 200 by 400 yards (180 by 370 m) had been built during the 1930s, and completed by 1935, by blasting the required space out of marl and possessed walls and roofs composed of 5 feet (1.5 m) thick reinforced concrete, as well as four retractable casemates and sixty-four strongpoints.

The Fort was equipped with six 120mm artillery pieces with a range of ten miles, two of which could traverse 360 degrees; sixteen 75mm artillery pieces; twelve 60mm high-velocity anti-tank guns; twenty-five twin-mounted machine-guns; and a number of anti-aircraft guns. One side of the fort faced the canal, whilst the other three faced land and were defended by minefields; deep ditches; a 20 feet (6.1 m) high wall; concrete pillboxes fitted with machine-guns; fifteen searchlights emplaced on top of the Fort; and 60mm anti-tank guns. A large number of tunnels ran beneath the Fort, connecting individual turrets to the command centre of the Fort and the ammunition stores. The Fort also possessed its own hospital and a number of living quarters for the garrison, as well as a power station that provided electricity to power the guns, provide internal and external illumination, and to power the wireless network and air-purifying system used by the garrison. Belgian plans did not call for the garrison of the fort and the attached defending forces to fight a sustained battle against an attacking force; it was assumed that sufficient warning of an attack would be given so that the detachment on the eastern side of the canal could be withdrawn, the bridges destroyed and the garrison ready to fight a delaying action. The defending force would then retire to the main defensive positions along the River Dyle, where they would link up with other Allied forces.

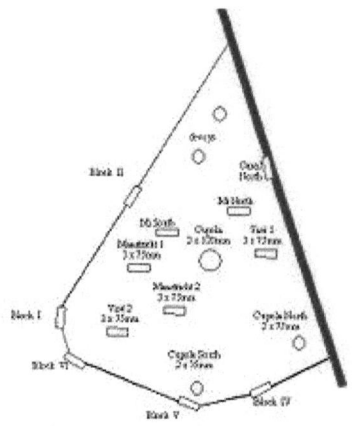

Map of Fort Eben-Emael

German Preparation

The airborne assault on Fort Eben Emael and the three bridges it helped protect was part of a much larger German airborne operation which involved the 7th Air Division and the 22nd Airlanding Division. The 7th Air Division, comprising three parachute regiments and one infantry regiment, was tasked with capturing a number of river and canal bridges that led to the Dutch defensive positions centered around Rotterdam, as well as an airfield at Waalhaven. The 22nd Airlanding Division, which was composed of two infantry regiments and a reinforced parachute battalion, was tasked with capturing a number of airfields in the vicinity of The Hague at Valkenburg, Ockenburg and Ypenburg. Once these airfields had been secured by the parachute battalion, the rest of the division would land with the aim of occupying the Dutch capital and capturing the entire Dutch government, the Royal Family and high-ranking members of the Dutch military. The division would also interdict all roads and railway lines in the area to impede the movement of Dutch forces. The intention of the German OKW was to use the two airborne divisions to create a corridor, along which the 18th Army could advance into the Netherlands without being impeded by destroyed bridges. General Kurt Student, who proposed the deployment of the two airborne divisions, argued that their presence would hold open the southern approaches to Rotterdam, prevent the movement of Dutch reserves based in north-west Holland and any French forces sent to aid the Dutch defenders, and deny the use of airfields to Allied aircraft, all of which would aid a rapid advance by the 18th Army. 400 Junkers Ju 52 transport aircraft would be used to deploy the parachute elements of the airborne troops, as well as transport the elements of the two airborne divisions not landing by parachute or glider.

The force tasked with assaulting the Fort and capturing the three bridges was formed from elements of the 7th Air Division and the 22nd Airlanding Division, and was named Sturmabteilung Koch (Assault Detachment Koch) after the leader of the force, Hauptmann Walter Koch. The force had been assembled in November 1939 and was primarily composed of parachutists from the 1st Parachute Regiment and engineers from the 7th Air Division, as well as a small group of Luftwaffe pilots. Although the force was composed primarily of parachutists, it was decided that the first landings by the force should be by glider. Adolf Hitler, who had taken a personal interest in the arrangements for the assault force, had ordered that gliders be used after being told by his personal pilot, Hanna Reitsch, that gliders in flight were nearly silent; it was believed that, since Belgian anti-aircraft defences used sound-location arrays and not radar, it would be possible to tow gliders near to the Dutch border and then release them, achieving a surprise attack as the Belgian defenders would not be able to detect them. Fifty DFS 230 transport gliders were supplied for use by the assault force, and then a period of intensive training began. A detailed study of the Fort, the bridges and the local area was made, and a replica of the area was constructed for the airborne troops to train in. Joint exercises between the parachutists and the glider pilots were carried out in the early spring of 1940, and a number of refinements made to the equipment and tactics to be used, such as barbed wire being added to the nose-skids of the gliders to reduce their landing run, and the airborne troops trained with flamethrowers and specialized explosives, the latter of which were so secret that they were only used on fortifications in Germany and not on fortifications in Czechoslovakia similar to Fort Eben Emael. Secrecy was also maintained in a number of other ways. When exercises were completed gliders and equipment would be broken down and taken away in furniture vans, the sub-units of the force were frequently renamed and moved from one location to another, unit badges and insignia were removed, and the airborne troops were not permitted to leave their barracks or to take leave.

German DFS 230 troop-carrying glider

Hauptmann Koch divided his force into four assault groups. Group Granite, under Oberleutnant Rudolf Witzig, composed of eighty-five men in eleven gliders whose task would be to assault and capture Fort Eben Emael; Group Steel, commanded by Oberleutnant Gustav Altmann, and formed of ninety-two men and nine gliders, would capture the Veldwezelt bridge; Group Concrete, commanded by Leutnant Gerhard Schächt and composed of ninety-six men in eleven gliders, would capture the Vroenhoven bridge; and Group Iron, under Leutnant Martin Schächter, composed of ninety men in ten gliders, who would capture the Cannes bridge. The crucial element for the assault force, and particularly Group Granite, was time. It was believed that the combination of a noiseless approach by the gliders used by the assault force, and the lack of a declaration of war by the German government, would give the attackers the element of surprise. However, German estimates believed that this would last, at the most, for sixty minutes, after which the superior numbers of the Belgian forces defending the Fort and the bridges, as well as any reinforcements sent to the area, would begin to come to bear against the relatively small number of lightly armed airborne troops. The German plan, therefore, was to eliminate within those sixty minutes as many anti-aircraft positions and individual cupolas and casemates as was possible, and at all costs to put out of action the long-range artillery pieces which covered the three bridges. The destruction of these guns was expected to be completed within ten minutes; within this time the airborne troops would have to break out of their gliders, cover the distance to the guns, fix the explosive charges to the barrels of the guns and detonate them, all while under enemy fire.

The finalized plan for the assault called for between nine and eleven gliders to land on the western bank of the Albert Canal by each of the three bridges just prior to 05:30 on 10 May, the time scheduled for Fall Gelb to begin. The groups assigned to assault the three bridges would overwhelm the defending Belgian troops, remove any demolition charges and then prepare to defend the bridges against an expected counter-attack. Forty minutes later, three Ju-52 transport aircraft would fly over each position, dropping a further twenty-four airborne troops as reinforcements as well as machine-guns and significant amounts of ammunition. Simultaneously, the force assigned to assault Fort Eben Emael was to land on top of the Fort in eleven gliders, eliminate any defenders attempting to repel them, cripple what artillery they could with explosive charges, and then prevent the Garrison from dislodging them. Having achieved their initial objectives of seizing the bridges and eliminate the long-range artillery pieces possessed by the Fort, the airborne troops would then defend their positions until the arrival of German ground forces.

Battle

For reasons of security, Sturmabteilung Koch was dispersed around several locations in the Rhineland until it received orders for the operation against Fort Eben-Emael and the three bridges to begin. Preliminary orders were received on 9 May, ordering the separated detachments to move to a pre-arranged concentration area, and shortly afterwards a second order arrived, informing the assault force that Fall Gelb was to begin at 05:25 on 10 May. At 04:30, forty-two gliders carrying the 493 airborne troops that formed the assault force were lifted off from two airfields in Cologne, the armada of gliders and transport aircraft turning south towards their objectives. The aircraft maintained strict radio silence, forcing the pilots to rely on a chain of signal fires that pointed towards Belgium; the radio silence also ensured that senior commanders of the assault force could not be informed that the tow-ropes on one of the gliders had snapped, forcing the glider to land inside Germany. Another pilot of a second glider released his tow-rope prematurely, and was unable to land near its objective. Both gliders were carrying troops assigned to Group Granite and were destined to assault Fort Eben Emael, thereby leaving the Group understrength; it also left it under the command of Oberleutnant Witzig's second-in-command, as Witzig was in one of the gliders forced to land. The remaining gliders were released from their tow-ropes twenty miles away from their objectives at an altitude of 7,000 feet (2,100 m), which was deemed high enough for the gliders to land by the three bridges and on top of the Fort, and also maintain a steep dive angle to further ensure they landed correctly. After the Ju-52's released the gliders and began turning away, Belgian anti-aircraft artillery positions detected them and opened fire. This alerted the defences in the area to the presence of the gliders.

Bridges

All nine gliders carrying the troops assigned to Group Steel landed next to the bridge at Veldwezelt at 05:20, the barbed-wire wrapped around the landing skids of the gliders succeeding in rapidly bringing the gliders to a halt.

The glider belonging to Leutnant Altmann had landed some distance from the bridge, and a second had landed directly in front of a Belgian pillbox, which began engaging both groups of airborne troops with small-arms fire. The non-commissioned officer in charge of the troops from the second glider hurled grenades at the pillbox whilst another of his men laid an explosive charge at the door to the pillbox and detonated it, allowing the bunker to be assaulted and removed as an obstacle. Simultaneously, Altmann gathered his troops and led them along a ditch running parallel to the Bridge until two men were able to reach the canal bank and climb onto the girders of the bridge and disconnect the demolition charges placed there by the Belgian garrison. Thus the airborne troops prevented the Belgians from destroying the bridge, though they still faced the rest of the Belgian defenders. The defenders held on until the a platoon of reinforcements arrived and forced them to retire to a nearby village. However, the assaulting force could not overcome two field-guns located five hundred metres from the bridge by small-arms fire, thus forcing Altmann to call for air support. Several Junkers Ju 87 Stukas responded and knocked out the guns. Group Steel was to be relieved by 14:30, but Belgian resistance delayed their arrival in strength until 21:30. During the fighting, the attacking force lost eight airborne troops dead and thirty wounded.

Photo of a German Junkers Ju 87 Stuka dive bomber, ca. 1940

Ten of the eleven gliders transporting Group Concrete landed next to the Vroenhoven bridge at 05:15, the eleventh glider having been hit by anti-aircraft fire en-route to the bridge and being forced to land prematurely inside Dutch territory. The gliders were engaged by heavy anti-aircraft fire as they landed, causing one of the gliders to stall in mid-air. The resulting crash severely wounded three airborne troops. The rest of the gliders landed without damage. One of the gliders landed near to the fortification housing the bridge detonators. This allowed the airborne troops to rapidly assault the position. They killed the occupants and tore out the wires connecting the explosives to the detonator set, ensuring the bridge could not be destroyed. The remaining Belgian defenders resisted fiercely by mounting several counter-attacks in an attempt to recapture the bridge. They were repelled with the aid of several machine-guns dropped by parachute to the airborne troops at 06:15. Constant Belgian attacks meant that Group Concrete were not withdrawn and relieved by an infantry battalion until 21:40. They suffered losses of seven dead and twenty-four wounded.

All but one of the ten gliders carrying the airborne troops assigned to Group Iron were able to land next to their objective, the bridge at Canne. Due to a navigation error by the pilots of the transport aircraft towing the gliders, one of the gliders was dropped in the wrong area. The other nine gliders were towed through heavy anti-aircraft fire and released at 05:35. As the gliders began to descend towards their objective, the bridge was destroyed by several demolition explosions set off by the Belgian garrison. Unlike the garrisons of the other two bridges, the Belgian defenders at Canne had been forewarned, as the German mechanized column heading for the bridge to reinforce Group Iron arrived twenty minutes ahead of schedule. Its appearance ruined any chance of a surprise assault and gave the defenders sufficient time to destroy the bridge. As the gliders came in to land, one was hit by anti-aircraft fire and crashed into the ground killing most of the occupants. The remaining eight landed successfully, and the airborne troops stormed the Belgian positions and eliminated the defenders.

By 05:50 the airborne troops had secured the area as well as the nearby village of Canne, but they were then subjected to a strong counter-attack which was only repulsed with the aid of air support from Stuka divebombers. The defenders launched several more counter-attacks during the night, ensuring that the airborne troops could not be relieved until the morning of 11 May. Group Iron suffered the heaviest casualties of all three assault groups assigned to capture the bridges with twenty-two dead and twenty-six wounded. One of the airborne troops assigned to the Group was taken prisoner by the Belgians. He was later freed by German forces at a British Prisoner of War camp at Dunkirk.

Fort Eben-Emael

A bridge leading to Fort Eben-Emael destroyed by the Belgian military, 23 May 1940

The nine remaining gliders transporting the airborne troops assigned to Group Granite successfully landed on the roof of Fort Eben-Emael, utilizing arrester parachutes to slow their descent and rapidly bring them to a halt. The airborne troops rapidly emerged from the gliders and began attaching explosive charges to those emplacements on the top of the Fort which housed the artillery pieces that could target the three captured bridges. In the southern part of the Fort, Objective No. 18, an artillery observation casemate housing three 75mm artillery pieces was damaged with a light demolition charge and then permanently destroyed with a heavier charge, which collapsed the casemates observation dome and part of the roof of the Fort itself. Objective No. 12, a traversing turret holding two more artillery pieces was also destroyed by airborne troops, who then moved to Objective No. 26, a turret holding another three 75mm weapons; although explosives were detonated against this and the airborne troops assigned to destroy it moved off, this proved to be premature as one of the guns was rapidly brought to bear against the attackers, who were forced to assault it for a second time to destroy it. Another pair of 75mm guns in a cupola were disabled, as was a barracks known to house Belgian troops. However, attempts to destroy Objective No. 24 proved to be less successful; the objective, twin turrets with heavy-calibre guns mounted on a rotating cupola, was too large for airborne troops from a single glider to destroy on their own, forcing troops from two gliders to be used. Shaped charges were affixed to the turrets and detonated, but whilst they shook the turrets they did not destroy them, and other airborne troops were forced to climb the turrets and smash the gun barrels.

One of the Fort Eben-Emael's casemates, "Maastricht 2"

In the northern section of the fort, similar actions were taking place, as the airborne troops raced to destroy or otherwise disable the fortifications housing artillery pieces. Objective No. 13 was a casemate housing multiple machine-guns whose arcs of fire covered the western side of the Fort; to destroy the casemate, the airborne troops used a flamethrower to force the Belgian soldiers manning the weapons to retreat, and then detonated shaped charges against the fortification to disable it. Another observation cupola fitted with machine-guns, Objective No. 19, was destroyed, but two further objectives, Nos. 15 and 16 were found to be dummy installations. Unexpected complications came from Objective No. 23, a retractable cupola housing two 75mm artillery pieces. It had been assumed that the weapons in this fortification could not stop the airborne assault, but this assumption was found to be false when the weapons opened fire, forcing the airborne troops in the area to go to cover. The rapid fire of the weapons led to air support being summoned, and a Stuka squadron bombed the cupola. Although the bombs did not destroy the cupola, the explosions did force the Belgians to retract it throughout the rest of the fighting. Any exterior entrances and exits located by the airborne troops were destroyed with explosives to seal the garrison inside the Fort, giving the garrison few opportunities to attempt a counter-attack. The airborne troops had achieved their initial objective of destroying or disabling the artillery pieces that the fort could have used to bombard the captured bridges, but they still faced a number of small cupolas and emplacements that had to be disabled. A number of these included anti-aircraft weapons and machine-guns.

Albert canal as seen from a Fort Eben-Emael machine gun position, 23 May 1940

As these secondary objectives were attacked, a single glider landed on top of the Fort, from which emerged Oberleutnant Rudolf Witzig. Once glider had landed in German territory, he had radioed for another tug, and it landed in the field with a replacement glider. Once the airborne troops with had broken down fences and hedges obstructing the aircraft, they had boarded the new glider and were towed through anti-aircraft fire to the fort. Having achieved their primary objectives of disabling the artillery pieces possessed by the fort, the airborne troops then held it against Belgian counter-attacks, which began almost immediately. These counter-attacks were made by Belgian infantry formations without artillery support and were uncoordinated. This allowed the airborne troops to repel them with machine-gun fire. Artillery from several smaller Forts nearby and Belgian field artillery units also targeted the airborne troops, but this too was uncoordinated and achieved nothing and often aided the airborne troops in repelling counter-attacks by Belgian infantry units. Patrols were also used to ensure that the garrison stayed in the interior of the fort and did not attempt to emerge and mount an attempt to retake the fort. Any attempt by the garrison to launch a counter-attack would have been stymied by the fact that the only possible route for such an attack was up a single, spiral staircase, and any embrasures looking out onto the Fort had either been captured or disabled. The plan for the assault had called for Group Granite to be relieved by 51st Engineer Battalion within a few hours of seizing the Fort, but the Group was not actually relieved until 7:00 on May 11. Heavy Belgian resistance, as well as several demolished bridges over the River Meuse, had forced the battalion to lay down new bridges, delaying it significantly. Once the airborne troops had been relieved, the battalion, in conjunction with an infantry regiment that arrived shortly after the engineers, mounted an attack on the main entrance to the fort. Faced with this attack, the garrison surrendered at 12:30, suffering sixty men killed and forty wounded. The Germans took more than a thousand Belgian soldiers into captivity. Group Granite suffered six killed and nineteen wounded.

Aftermath

Fallschirmjäger of Sturmabteilung Koch

The airborne assault on the three bridges and Fort Eben-Emael had been an overall success for the Fallschirmjäger of Sturmabteilung Koch; the artillery pieces possessed by Fort Eben-Emael had been disabled, and two of the three bridges designated to be captured by the sub-units of Sturmabteilung Koch had been captured before they could be destroyed. The capture of the bridges, and the neutralization of the artillery pieces in the Fort allowed infantry and armour from the 18th Army to bypass other Belgian defences and enter the heart of Belgium. In a postwar publication, General Kurt Student wrote of the operation, and the efforts of Group Granite in particular, that "It was a deed of exemplary daring and decisive significance [...] I have studied the history of the last war and the battles on all fronts. But I have not been able to find anything among the host of brilliant actions—undertaken by friend or foe—that could be said to compare with the success achieved by Koch's Assault Group." A number of officers and non-commissioned officers were awarded the Knight's Cross of the Iron Cross for their participation in the operation, including Lieutenant Rudolf Witzig who led the assault on Fort Eben-Emael in the absence of Koch. Sturmabteilung Koch was expanded after the end of Fall Gelb to become 1st Battalion of the newly formed 1st Airlanding Assault Regiment, which itself consisted of four battalions of Fallschirmjaeger trained as a gliderborne assault force. Hauptmann Koch was promoted to the rank of Major for his part in the operation and assumed command of the 1st Battalion.
Source (edited): "http://en.wikipedia.org/wiki/Battle_of_Fort_Eben-Emael"

Battle of Hannut

The **Battle of Hannut** (not to be confused with the Battle of Gembloux Gap) was a Second World War battle fought during the Battle of Belgium which took place between 12 and 14 May 1940 at Hannut, Belgium. At the time, it was the largest tank battle yet to occur.

The primary purpose of the Germans was to tie down the strongest elements of the 1st French Army and remove it from the German's Army Group A main thrust through the Ardennes, as laid out in the German operational plan *Fall Gelb*, or "Case Yellow", by *General* Erich von Manstein. The German breakout of the Ardennes was scheduled for 15 May, five days after the German attacks on the Netherlands and Belgium. The delay was to entice the Allies into believing the main thrust would, like the Schlieffen Plan in World War I, come through Belgium and then down into France. When the Allied armies advanced into Belgium, they would be tied down by German offensive operations in eastern Belgium at Hannut and Gembloux. With the 1st French Army flank exposed, the German could thrust to the English Channel which would encircle and destroy the Allied forces. For the French Army, the plan in Belgium was to prepare defences for a prolonged defence at Gembloux, some 21 miles to the west of Hannut. The French sent two armoured divisions to Hannut, to delay the German advance and give strong French forces time to prepare a defence at Gembloux. Regardless of what happened at Hannut, the French planned to fall back on Gembloux.

The Germans reached the Hannut area just two days after the start of the invasion of Belgium. The French won a series of delaying tactical engagements at Hannut and fell back on Gembloux as planned. However, the Germans succeeded in tying down substantial Allied forces at Hannut which might have participated in the decisive blow through the Ardennes.

The Germans failed to neutralise the French 1st Army completely at Hannut, despite inflicting significant casualties and it withdrew to Gembloux. There, the French once again scored tactical successes at the battle of Gembloux during the 14—15 May. In the aftermath of that battle, although seriously damaged, the French 1st Army was able retreat to Lille, where it delayed the *Wehrmacht* and assisted in the British Expeditionary Force' escape from Dunkirk.

Background

Allied intentions

The Allied supreme commander General Maurice Gamelin committed his First Army Group, under General Gaston Billotte, and its strongest Army, the French 1st Army with the fully mechanised *Corps de Cavalerie* (Cavalry Corps), commanded by General René-Jacques-Adolphe Prioux, to advance into Belgium to support the large but more lightly equipped Belgian Army. Gamelin expected the German attack to break the Belgian defences at the Albert Canal line rapidly—the Belgians had in any case indicated they would after four days withdraw to the planned allied front in central Belgium, the "Dyle Line" between Antwerp and Namur—and sought to quickly establish an entrenched front line centred on Gembloux, just north of Namur, to check what Gamelin foresaw as the main enemy effort (*Schwerpunkt*) of the campaign: an attempt to break through the "Gembloux Gap" between the rivers Dyle and Meuse with a concentration of armoured forces. As Belgium, the Netherlands, and Luxembourg would remain neutral until the German invasion of those countries (*Fall Gelb*), it had proven impossible to adequately prepare positions for the French 1st Army. Therefore the Cavalry Corps was given the mission to execute a delaying battle, somewhere between Gembloux and Maastricht (the likely crossing-point, where the Albert Canal connected to it, over the eastern bend of the Meuse), to prevent the enemy from reaching the Gembloux area until the eighth day of an invasion and to allow the 1st Army sufficient time to dig in.

The Cavalry Corps had been created on 26 December 1939, containing both then existing armoured divisions of the Cavalry, the *1re Division Légère Mécanique* ("1st Mechanised Light Division") and the *2e DLM*. On 26 March 1940 however, 1st DLM was given the mission, in case of an invasion, to establish a connection with the Dutch Army near Breda; this experienced active division was therefore removed from the Cavalry Corps. It was replaced by the *3e DLM*, recently constituted on 1 February, manned with reservists and still insufficiently trained. Nevertheless, Prioux still considered his forces sufficient to either contest a river-crossing at Maastricht, or wage a manoeuvre battle or, as a third alternative, defend an improvised line. He was at liberty to choose any option, provided the enemy was kept from Gembloux long enough. He decided to keep all possibilities open and act as the situation would demand.

German intentions

General Hoepner commanded Army Corps XVI at the Battle of Hannut and the Gembloux gap offensive

The German plan for this sector called for an assault by airborne and shock troops to take Fort Eben-Emael and the Meuse and Albert Canal bridges, thus opening a way through the Dutch and Belgian defences for the *4. Panzerdivision* (4th Panzer Division), and bring the Albert Canal defensive line to a premature collapse. Once this breach was made, General Erich Hoepner's XVI Army Corps, and Army Group B would assume control of the 4th Panzer Division, the 3rd Panzer Division and the 20th Motorised Infantry Divisions. Hoepner's mission was to quickly launch his Corps from the bridgehead, seize the area around Gembloux before the French infantry divisions could entrench themselves there, and by thus conforming to the worst fears of the French High Command draw all modern Allied forces and their reserves to the north, away from the main thrust through the Ardennes. This would enable the Wehrmacht to cut the French First Army, the BEF and the Belgiums off by a swift advance to the English Channel leading to a giant encirclement. The action was basically a feint to tie down the Allies in the north so they could not interfere with the main thrust through the Ardennes.

Opposing forces

Allied forces

The Battle of Hannut became the largest tank battle of the campaign. The French DLMs had two *Brigades Légères Mécaniques* each, one of these, the "combat" brigade, contained two tank regiments, each regiment having a medium tank squadron equipped with the SOMUA S35, and a light tank squadron fielding the Hotchkiss H35. Its organic strength was 44 S35s and 43 H35s; also eight armoured command vehicles were present. The other brigade contained a reconnaissance regiment, equipped with 44 Panhard 178 armoured cars organised in two squadrons, and a mechanised infantry regiment equipped with 126 Laffly S20TL personnel carriers. Three organic AMR (*Automitrailleuse de Reconnaissance*) squadrons of 22 tanks each were also included as were three armoured command vehicles. The *2e DLM* used AMR 35 tanks for this rôle, but as the production of this light tank had been discontinued, *3e DLM* employed H35s instead.

SOMUA S35 at the Bovington Tank Museum. It outmatched the Panzer I to IIIs in terms of armour.

Each DLM thus had an organic strength of 240 tanks and 44 Panhards, for a total of 176 SOMUA S35s, 238 Hotchkiss H35s, 66 AMR 35s and 88 P 178s, including the organic matériel reserve.

The *3e DLM* used *modifié 39* versions, a swifter, improved of the H35s, that today is often referred to as the "H 39", but also had a single AMR squadron of 22 vehicles of the slower original batch of four hundred, that were exclusively present in *2e DLM*. Most Hotchkiss tanks of both versions were fitted with the short, Long 21, 37 mm gun, which proved a poor antitank weapon. Some platoon and squadron commander's vehicles had been fitted with the more powerful Long 35 SA 38 37 mm gun, totalling about a fifth of the total number of Hotchkiss tanks.

The organisation of *2e DLM* was: *3e BLM* as a combat brigade, with *13e Dragons* and *29e Dragon* tank regiments; the second brigade was *4e BLM* with *8e Cuirassiers* reconnaissance regiment and *1er Dragons* mechanised infantry regiment. The *3e DLM* had *5e BLM* with *1er Cuirassiers* and *2e Cuirassiers* tank regiments and *6e BLM* with *12e Cuirassiers* reconnaissance regiment and *11e Dragons* mechanised infantry regiment.

German forces

Panzer I Ausf. A during the invasion of Belgium.

Like their French counterparts the German armoured divisions each had an armoured brigade (*Panzer-Brigade*) with two tank regiments (*Panzer-Regimente*). The latter were divided into two tank battalions (*Panzer-Abteilungen*); each tank battalion had, apart from a staff company, two light companies of nineteen battle tanks, in theory mainly equipped with the *Panzerkampfwagen* III, and a medium company of fifteen battle tanks using the *Panzerkampfwagen* IV. Due to a shortage of these types, the positions were actually in majority filled with the light *Panzerkampfwagen* II and even *Panzerkampfwagen* I. The exact numbers of each type on 10 May available to the German armoured divisions are known: 3rd Pz. Div. had 314 battle tanks in its *3. Panzer-Brigade* consisting of *5.* and *6. Panzer-Regiment*: 117 PzKpfw Is, 129 PzKpfw IIs, 42 PzKpfw IIIs and 26 PzKpfw IVs; 4th Pz. Div. had 304 battle tanks in its *5. Panzer-Brigade* consisting of *35.* and *36. Panzerregiment*: 135 PzKpfw Is, 105 PzKpfw IIs, 40 PzKpfw IIIs and 24 PzKpfw IVs. *XVI. Armeekorps* thus had a total of 618 tanks: 252 PzKpfw Is, 234 PzKpfw IIs, 82 PzKpfw IIIs and 50 PzKpfw IVs. Besides these battle tanks, 3rd Pz. Div. had 27 *Befehlspanzer* tracked command vehicles with only machine-gun armament and 4th Pz. Div. ten. Each division also had about 56 armoured cars. Most PzKpfw IIs of *XVI Armeekorps* had not yet been uparmoured to the new 30 mm standard and were thus vulnerable to even the French 37 mm L/21 gun.

As the French mechanised infantry regiments had three mechanised infantry battalions, total infantry strength of the *Corps de Cavalerie* (CC) was six battalions. *XVI. Armeekorps* had seven motorised infantry battalions. The French units were only lightly equipped with antitank-guns: twelve 25 mm and eight 47 mm SA 37 guns per division; and anti-aircraft guns: six 25 mm guns per division. Also, there was an imbalance in artillery: the French Mechanised Light Divisions each had 36 pieces against 68 (including 24 7.5 cm *leichtes Infanteriegeschütz* 18) per *Panzerdivision*. This was not set off by Corps artillery; the Germans had four attached artillery regiments and a heavy battery; the French CC only two 75 mm field gun regiments (and a group of twelve 25 mm antitank-guns) as corps troops.

The specialized *VIII. Fliegerkorps* of the *Luftwaffe*, with some 300 Junkers 87 dive bombers and 42 Henschel Hs 123 biplanes, plus some 130 Messerschmitt 109 fighter aircraft, stood ready to support the *Panzers*. The *IV. Fliegerkorps* and *IX. Fliegerkorps* added some 280 medium bombers and over 500 Messerschmitt 109 and Messerschmitt Bf 110 heavy fighters, some of which would also be at Hoepner's disposal.

Prelude to engagement

Prioux's mistake

Billotte suggested to Prioux that he might force his armour further east to support the Belgian Army. But Prioux, unimpressed by the Belgian defence and fearing to concentrate his force in the open beneath a dominant *Luftwaffe*, preferred to deploy his dragoons and supporting arms further back in a line of strong points, with his tanks behind them to counter attack enemy penetrations. Billotte accepted his decision and, impressed by the need for haste, added that the First Army Group would advance by day as well as by night, despite the threat of the *Luftwaffe*, in order to reach Gembloux. Thus Prioux need stall the Panzers only until the dawn of 14 May.

At 11:00 A.M. on 11 May, Billotte diverted most of the French 23rd Fighter Group (*Fighter Groupement 23*) to cover the advance of the First Army and its neighbouring units. After more fighters had been removed for bomber escort missions, few fighters were left to cover the cavalry. The Allied bombers concentrated on retarding the dangerous advance of Hoepner's Panzers. Prioux's ground reconnaissances fell back before the Panzers, toward the main body of French cavalry, which was established in strongpoints along a 40 km front with the 2d DLM from Huy on the Meuse and north, then westward along the Mehaigne creek. The 3d DLM formed a front from the area of Crehen to Orp and then northward along the Petite Gette stream to the area of Tirlemont. The battleground which Prioux chose consisted of a plateau with occasional woods, a dense road network, extended localities and a few isolated large farms. The Mehaigne and Petite Gette were small streams flowing within two-to-three-meter-deep rock cuts with many crossing points, often fordable by tracked vehicles, and offering good cover for would-be infiltrators. But the key terrain feature was the ridge running from Hannut through Crehen and Merdorp. North of the ridge, the Petite Gette flowed north into the Escaut River, south of it, the Mehaigne flowed south into the Meuse. This ridge formed a natural corridor for mechanized forces.

By placing the 3d DLM on a 17 km front, only 11 km were partially covered by anti-tank obstacles. Prioux was straining the limits of French doctrine. The French cavalry manual of 1939 (General Langlois was one its authors and was now commanding the 3d DLM) had considered the case of a DLM assigned to mask a breach in the front until reinforcements could arrive. In such a case, the manual ruled, command would be decentralised. The division should place a combined-arms force on each flank of possible penetration. Then the commander would move his artillery and his reserves to maintain a continuous line of fire. But, if the enemy attacked in force along the whole front, this defence transforms itself into a manouvre of retreat. The manual added that a DLM could retreat on a front of no more than 10 to 15 km in average terrain. In the event of the front's extension, the absence of anti-tank obstacles, and a formidable enemy, a withdrawal should be made. French doctrine warned that on a wide front on open terrain against massed armour, the DLM was to abandon the decentralised defence and to concentrate its forces for action. Prioux did not follow these directions.

French deployment

The French command articulated its cavalry front on May 11. On the left, the 3d DLM under General Langlois, its front divided into northern and southern sectors. The northern sector, commanded by Colonel Dodart des Loges, had, from north to south, the 12th Cuirassiers (division reconnaissance regiment), in touch with British and Belgian cavalry in the Tirlemont area, then a line of two battalions of the 11th Dragoon Regiment; the 3d Battalion holding six kilometers along the Petite Gette around Opheylissem, with 21 Hotchkisses plus another such squadron from the 1st Cuirassiers battalion and supported by 21 75 mm guns from the Cavalry Corps reserve; and the 2d Battalion holding five kilometers along the Petite Gette southward to Orp, similarly with its own Hotchkisses plus another squadron from the 1st Cuirassiers and supported by 12 75mm artillery from the 76th artillery. Behind this sector stood one squadron of SOMUA tanks of the 1st Cuirassiers at Marilles. General de Lafont commanded the five kilometer southern sector of the division astride the dangerously open terrain facing Hannut. Lafont had the 1st Battalion of the 11th Dragoons in strongpoints at Thisnes, Wansin, and Crehen, with their Hotchkiss squadrons plus an additional Hotchkiss squadron each in Crehen and Thisnes from the 2d Cuirassiers, supported by 21 75 mm artillery guns and 12 105 mm guns from the 76th Artillery. One SOMUA squadron of the 1st Cuirassiers at Jauche and two such squadrons from the 2d Cuirassiers at Jandrenouille and Merdorp formed the sector reserve. South of Crehen the 2d DLM was positioned, covered along almost the whole of its front by the Mehaigne creek, down to Huy on the Meuse river.

Battle on 12 May

Morning actions

On 12 May *4. Panzerdivision* raced to seize their first objective, Hannut, reaching the area that morning. General Hoepner ordered the 3rd and 4th Panzer Divisions (3rd Pz. Div. and 4th Pz. Div.) to concentrate on and secure Hannut to secure the 6th Army's flank. Noting his lack of fuel and his divisions artillery and infantry support that had not yet caught up with the armour, which made an immediate assault on Hannut risky, Major-General Stever of the 4th Pz. Div. requested an air-drop of fuel. Concluding that he was only facing one French battalion, he engaged the French defences. That morning the 4th Pz. Div. made contact with a French Armoured force of some 25 tanks. The 4th Pz. Div. claimed seven of the French tanks for no losses.

Allied air units also concentrated on his unit, which could have made Stever's mission more difficult. The RAF sent over 38 bombers, losing 22. The Arme de l'air sent two expeditions, one including 18 of its Breguet 693 bombers on their maiden mission, losing eight. The 85 Messerschmitt 109s of *Jagdgeschwader 27* (Fighter Wing 27) flew 340 sorties that day, claiming 26 Allied aircraft for the loss of four fighters. German anti-aircraft artillery (AAA) claimed another 25. But that afternoon General Georges suddenly ordered air priority away from the Belgian plain to the threatened center of his front further south in the Sedan area. Prioux's cavalry formations now had little air cover.

Having surrendered the initiative and with only limited air reconnaissance, Prioux could only wait to see where the Panzers would concentrate. His right flank he anchored on the Meuse. He held Huy with two battalions of motorised heavy infantry plus some dragoons and artillery. His left was in touch with British light cavalry and parts of the Belgian Cavalry Corps delaying the enemy along the axis St. Trond-Tirlemont. German armoured cars followed by infantry infiltrations probed toward Tirlemont that afternoon, leading the French Cavalry Corps to order a squadron of tanks plus one of the divisional reconnaissance groups at its disposal to the area. British reinforcements also reached the scene. The German effort was essentially a reconnaissance and diversionary probe. The main preoccupation of both sides was the open area around Hannut.

On the ground, Stever's 35th Panzer Regiment advancing toward Hannut ran into fierce resistance. The French armour was deployed under cover and during the battle counter-attacked several times. The French forces then yielded Hannut without a fight. German forces attempted to outflank the town, unaware of the retreat. Some 50 light Panzers ran into the French strongpoint at Crehen. French defences equipped with 21 Hotchkiss tanks of the 2d Cuirassiers, supported by parts of the 76th Artillery Regiment plus fire from the nearby 2d DLM. The dragoons lost heavily, but it was the Hotchkisses which carried the burden of the defence, despite the loss of their commander. Firing from prepared positions, German medium tanks attempted to pin down the French while the light tanks moved around the French position. The main French forced retreated to Medorp. The encircled 2d Cuirassiers were freed by an armoured counter attack from the 2DLM. SOMUA S35s breached the German line and the French units broke out, suffering heavy losses in the process. The right flank of the 4th Pz. Div. was now dangerously exposed.

Evening action

Rushing from the German staging area at Oreye, some 11 km to the northeast of Hannut, the 3rd Pz. Div. moved up to cover this threat. At 16:30 P.M, German 6th Army requested air reconnaissance. The *Luftwaffe* reported French armour at Orp and motorised units at Gembloux. Reichenau, commander of the German 6th Army, ordered Hoepner to send XVI Corps forward to Gembloux to prevent the French from organising a defence, but Hoepner continued to worry about his stretched supply lines and especially his exposed flanks. His neighbouring IV Corps had elements in the St. Trond area probing toward Tirlemont, worrying Prioux, but the XXVII Corps was still held up north of Liege 38 km east of Hannut, leaving Hoepner's southern flank exposed.

The German solution was to build an advance guard of one Panzer battalion and one rifle battalion supported by two artillery groups to push forward to Perwez, 18 km south west of Hannut, if possible. But Stever ordered his guard that if they met serious resistance the attack was to be halted. The force advanced under heavy air and artillery cover against the French strongpoint at Thisnes, and simply ignored the French counterattack at Crehen in its rear. The streets of Thisnes were barricaded. Heavy French artillery and other fire met the attack, stopping the tank company on point. The remainder of the German force flanked the French position to their right, though poor visibility hampered the movement. The guard finally reached the western edge of the town, only to meet strong artillery fire from the neighbouring French strongpoint in Wansin which continued to increase. The force was ordered to regroup its tanks and riflemen and to secure a perimeter. But before this could be done, French SOMUAs counter attacked knocking out the Panzer Regiment commander's tank. After hard fighting both French and German tanks pulled back in the darkness, stumbling into each other on occasion. The French retreated to Merdorp and the Panzers to the Hannut area.

At 20:00 Stever spoke to Hoepner, telling him he was certain two French mechanised divisions were before him, one to his front and one behind the Mehaigne river. Both agreed to mount a major offensive the next day. According to the plan the 4th Pz. Div. would concentrate to Gembloux's right and operate jointly with the 3rd Panzer, which would receive air support from *Fliegerkorps VIII*.

The Germans attacked that night, testing the French defences. The French strongpoint at Wansin fought all night against German riflemen, finally withdrawing in the early hours of 13 May. The front of the 3rd DLM remained, holding positions near Tienen, Jandrenouille and Merdorp. The 2nd DLM also held its original front. The only breach of the line occurred at Winson, where the 2nd DLM met the 3rd DLM. Hoepner had failed to take his objective. "On the very first day, French armour — contrary to German reports — definitely emerged victorious".

Battle on 13 May

Morning actions

To the south-east of the plain, German forces began their assault over the Meuse River: the Wehrmacht's principal effort. To the north, General Hoepner launched spoiling attacks and tied down the powerful French First Army, so that it could not intervene. Hoepner believed the newly arrived 3rd Pz. Div. had only weak enemy forces before it; the 4th Pz. Div. on the other hand, he believed, faced strong French mechanised forces at Hannut and Thisnes—which the French had in fact already abandoned—and possibly a second French mechanised division south of the Mehaigne. The Luftwaffe struck in the late morning to soften the enemy defences. The 3rd Pz. Div. advanced on Thorembais. The 4th Panzer was to move in parallel on Perwez, against an expected strong Belgian anti-tank line. XVI Army Corps thus fell back on the 6th Army's instruction to push immediately on Gembloux.

The French 12th Cuirassiers and to the south the 3rd Battalion of the 11th Dragoons, fought off waves of German infantry supported by armoured vehicles. The German 18th Infantry Division still penetrated their positions. The French command planned to counter-attack with tanks from the 1st Cuirassiers unit to restore their lines, but dropped those plans due to developments on the rest of the 3rd DLM's front. In the afternoon the French command ordered a retreat. The Allied force escaped as the German infantry was too slow in following up their success. The 2nd DLM was positioned just south of the planned axis of Hoepner's attack. In the early morning the 2nd DLM sent some 30 SOMUA S-35s from the Mehaigne to the line Merdorp-Crehen to relieve the pressure on the 3rd DLM. The attack was repulsed by heavy enemy tank and anti-tank fire near Crehen with crippling losses. General Bougrain, commanding the 2nd DLM, signalled enemy infiltrations and attacks by armoured cars over the Mehaigne river at Moha and Wanze, just north of Huy, attacks which threatened to cut off the large Belgian garrison in Huy. Bougrain diverted his tank reserves to try and retrieve the situation. At 15:00 a French reconnaissance aircraft reported large concentrations of German armour south-east of Crehen. The 2nd DLM no longer had reserves available to intervene.

Bougrain's Dragoons and motorised infantry were strung out in a series of isolated strongpoints and thus were vulnerable to infiltration. Bougrain refused the offer of the Belgian III Corps, retreating through his front from the Liege area, to reinforce his troops on the Mehaigne river. Prioux's lack of attention to French defensive doctrine and concentration had allowed decentralised command to continue which damaged the French operational performance which created problems for the French defence.

The German command for its part, worried by the potential of the 2d DLM to interfere with its main attack, juggled force marching infantry units between its XVI and XXVII Corps and scraped together four units from the 35th, 61st, and 269th Infantry Division advancing via Liege, along with air support and some armoured cars. These forces infiltrated between the French strongpoints north of Huy and drew out Bougrain's armour. This critical German successtying down French armour with infantry freed Hoepner to concentrate against

Prioux's front west of Hannut. Had Bougrain concentrated his armour for an advance to the north or northeast, he might have caused untold problems for the German plan. But Prioux gave him no such mission.

The real focus of the battle on 13 May lay west of Hannut. An order arrived from the 6th Army to Hoepner, not only to break through to Gembloux, but to pursue the enemy west of that position. Hoepner concentrated all of his Corps's Panzer and rifle battalions, including about 560 operational tanks, aided on their right by the 18th Infantry Division of the IV Corps, on a front of some 12 kilometers. The 3rd Panzer on the north facing Marilles and Orp, the 4th Panzer facing Thisnes and Merdorp. The 3rd Panzer Brigade of the 3rd Panzer Division moved out at about 11:30. with its 5th Panzer Regiment on he right and its 6th on the left, the Brigade Commander moved forward with the 5th Regiment. By noon the tanks were in action in the barricaded and mined towns along the Petite Gette river. After 90 minutes of heavy fighting, both Panzer regiments succeeded in pushing elements of the French defenders over the stream, the 5th before Marilles, the 6th at Orp. The German command ordered most of the 6th Regiment to turn south toward Jandrain and Jandrenouille, where the terrain was more favourable and they could aid the 4th Panzer Division. Operating on the east and west bank of the Petite Gette, the 6th Regiment ran into French armour in the Orp area, and was then attacked by further French armour. The German battalions combined to defeat the attack.

Tank battle at Orp

The German forces attacked in the afternoon. The 3rd Pz. Div. on the north facing Marilles and Orp, the 4th Pz. Div. facing Thisnes and Merdorp. The 5th and 6th Panzer Brigade of the 3rd Panzer Division faced an attack by French armour, and both sides clashed while on the offensive. The Panzers were numerically superior and could be seen moving in large formations while the French operated in small groups and fired more slowly. From 15:00 to 15:48 the 3rd Panzer Brigade issued repeated, urgent calls for anti-tank units and the Luftwaffe to deal with French tanks. The 2nd Battalion, 5th Panzer Regiment, still opposite Marilles, suddenly found itself attacked in the flank and rear by "superior" French armoured forces. The 3rd Panzer Brigade war diary recorded the 15 minutes during which the 2nd Battalion stood alone. The 1st Battalion, 5th Panzer Regiment, seeing victory on the left, sent the 1st Battalion back to his right, bringing the fight before Marilles to a successful conclusion at about 16:00. As the riflemen secured Orp, the Panzers put out an urgent call for 37 and 75 mm ammunition.

That morning the strongpoints of the 2d Battalion, 11th Dragoons suffered serious losses to air and artillery bombardment, while German motorcyclists followed by armoured cars searched for infiltration and crossing points. From about 11:30, the 3d DLM signalled some 80 Panzers opposite Marilles, some 100 before Orp. The dragoons defended their strongpoints supported by their organic Hotchkiss squadron, but their resistance began to crumple at about 13:30 as German numbers and lack of munitions told.

Colonel Dodart des Loges, commanding the northern sector of the 3rd DLM front, ordered a retreat, As the remaining dragoons withdrew, their Hotchkiss H35 tanks together with two Hotchkiss squadrons from the 1st Cuirassiers counter-attacked. The French pushed the German armour back to the stream. Losses were about even, the French claiming six Panzers for the loss of four. Colonel de Vernejoul commanding the 1st Cuirassiers dispatched 36 SOMUA S-35s to halt German armour advancing from Orp to Jandrain. German armoured forces then surprised the French as they attacked. An equal number of Panzers attacked from cover defeating the French attack.

This offensive was the principal effort of the 3rd DLM to check the 3rd Pz. Div. The 2nd DLM launched raids against the still vulnerable flanks of the 4th Pz. Div., and some small groups of French tanks broke through but were quickly dealt with by the German 654th Anti-tank battalion, attached to the 4 Pz. Div. Apart from these isolated and sporadic raids the 2nd DLM did not make any further attempts to attack the 4th Pz. Div.'s flank.

Afternoon actions

In the afternoon the 4th Pz. Div. began an assault on Medorp. As the French artillery opened fire and German artillery responded, the French pushed armour into the abandoned town and skillfully changed position making the Panzers struggle to strike their targets. The German tanks decided to bypass the town around its left flank, but this exposed the German infantry who were forced to give ground against encroaching French armour. The Panzers quickly did a u-turn and engaged the French in the open. Initially the French held the advantage due to their superior armour and firepower, but German tactics of *schwerpunkt*, concentrating their armour on the vital point, began to tell. Small groups of French infantry infiltrated and attacked from the rear but German infantry crushed any resistance.

At this point the 3rd Pz. Div. and 4th Pz. Div. were advancing to Jandrain. Outside the town a bitter tank battle took place. The Panzers prevailed through numbers and reported 22 French SOMUA S-35s totally destroyed. The German forces secured the area and town. German forces reported taking 400 prisoners, and capturing four and five tanks. The French forces, the 2nd and 3rd DLM began a general retreat westward. The Panzer Divisions, no longer fearing an attack to their flanks, advanced and engaged the remnants of the enemy in the evening. The 3rd Panzer Brigade claimed a tally for the day of 54 French tanks knocked out, 36 by the 5th Panzer Regiment, 18 by its sister unit; 3rd Panzer Regiment. Its own losses were listed as "slight". The 6th Panzer regiment reported a provisional loss total of only two tanks. The Germans suffered many more tanks disabled, but as the battlefield was secured a great many were repaired. The remainder of the 3rd DLM was in line behind the Belgian antitank obstacle on the front Beauvechain-La Bruyere-Pietrebais-Incourt-Perwez. The next morning the 2nd DLM fell back into line south of Perwez.

Battle on 14 May

Attack on Perwez

The German attack on Perwez came in the morning of 14 May. General Stumpff's 3rd Pz. Div. was to engage the new Allied line near Gembloux, whilst General Stever and the 4th Pz. Div. were to break through its centre at Perwez. Hoepner ordered the attack to commence without infantry support, but could not break through the French positions. The 4th Pz. Div. engaged French armour, which resisted heavily in wooded areas around Perwez. After hard fighting the French defences were destroyed with the help of German infantry. The French First Army had redistributed and spread its tank battalions behind the infantry. Spread out and unsupported, they were defeated by the concentration of numerically superior German combined arms teams. The 3rd Pz. Div. was halted due to fierce resistance from 2nd DLM. Bitter fighting resulted and the appearance of large numbers of French tanks panicked the German Command into thinking a major counter-attack was developing, when in fact they were just rearguard actions. Both sides suffered significant losses in armour, but as night fell the 2nd DLM halted rearguard actions and the German Command regained its composure. The Allied forces had gained themselves time to reorganise their forces in response to another major German assault on 15 May.

Aftermath

The German PzKpfw III and IV were the only German tanks capable of matching the SOMUA S35 in battle. The SOMUA S35 was generally considered to be the most formidable tank during the campaign in the west. Despite being outnumbered by odds of two to one, the German forces still managed to defeat the qualitative and numerical superiority of the French. The Germans saving grace was their superior tactical deployment. Using radio and mobility they constantly outmanoeuvred the French, who used rigid, static positioning as in the First World War. The French tanks could not communicate with such fluidity or rapidity. Thus tactical and operational expedience was lost, and prevented effective coordination. The German tanks also had more crew members. The Commander could concentrate on command tasks, while the French commanders had to act as gunner and assistant gunner as well.

The German plan failed to forestall the French 1st Army at Gembloux, despite their victory over the 3rd DLM. Still, Hoepner's advance to the Belgian plain tied down the Cavalry Corps and part of the French First Army while the decisive German assault succeeded across the Meuse to the south-east. The Germans had hoped that Hoepner's panzers and their neighbouring corps would tie down and neutralise the threat of the First Army. However on 15 May, forces of the First Army, properly settled into position, checked the *Panzerwaffe* which gained them time and space to manoeuvre. In the end it was the First Army which, sacrificing itself, held up the bulk of the Panzers which had broken through to the Southeast, enabling the British Expeditionary Force and other French units to escape from Dunkirk.

Source (edited): "http://en.wikipedia.org/wiki/Battle_of_Hannut"

Battle of the Scheldt

The **Battle of the Scheldt** was a series of military operations of the First Canadian Army, led by Lieutenant General Guy Simonds. The battle took place in northern Belgium and southwestern Netherlands during World War II from 2 October-8 November 1944

By September 1944, it had become urgent for the Allies to clear both banks of the Scheldt estuary in order to open the port of Antwerp to Allied shipping, thus easing logistical burdens in their supply lines stretching hundreds of miles from Normandy eastward to the Siegfried Line. Since the Allied forces had landed in Normandy, France on D-Day, 6 June 1944, the British Second Army had pushed forward into the Low Countries and captured Brussels and Antwerp, the latter with its ports still intact. But the advance halted with the British in possession of Antwerp, while the Germans still controlled the Scheldt Estuary.

Nothing was done about the blocked Antwerp ports during September because most of the strained Allied resources were allocated to Operation Market Garden, a bold plan for a single thrust into Germany which began on 17 September. In the meantime, German forces in the Scheldt were able to deploy to meet them.

In early October, after Market Garden had failed with heavy losses, Allied forces led by the First Canadian Army set out to bring the Antwerp ports under control. But the well-established German defenders staged an effective delaying action. Complicated by the waterlogged terrain, the Battle of the Scheldt proved to be a challenging campaign in which the losses suffered by the Canadians exacerbated another conscription crisis.

After five weeks of difficult fighting, the First Canadian Army, bolstered by attached troops from several other countries, was successful in clearing the Scheldt after numerous amphibious assaults, obstacle crossings, and costly assaults over open ground. Both land and water were mined, and the Germans defended their line of retreat with artillery and snipers.

The Allies finally cleared the port areas on 8 November at a cost of 12,873 Allied casualties (killed, wounded, or missing), half of them Canadians.

Once the German defenders were no longer a threat, it was an additional three weeks before the first ship carrying Allied supplies was able to unload in Antwerp (on November 29, 1944) due to the necessity of de-mining the harbors.

Opening the Scheldt

On 12 September 1944, the First Canadian Army under temporary command of Lieutenant-General Guy Simonds was given the task of clearing the Scheldt. Under command at that time was II Canadian Corps, with the Polish 1st Armoured Division, British 49th and 52nd Divisions attached, as well as British I Corps.

The plan for opening the Scheldt estuary involved four main operations conducted over daunting geography.
- The first task was to clear the area north of Antwerp and secure access to South Beveland.
- Second was to clear the Breskens pocket north of the Leopold Canal ("Operation Switchback").
- Third, dubbed "Operation Vitality", was the capture of South Beveland.
- The final phase would be the capture of Walcheren Island ("Operation Infatuate"), which had been fortified into a powerful German stronghold. As part of the Atlantic Wall, Walcheren Island was considered to be the "strongest concentration of defences the Nazis had ever constructed."

Column of Alligator amphibious vehicles passing Terrapin amphibious vehicles on the Scheldt river, October 1944.

On 21 September, the 4th Canadian (Armoured) Division moved north roughly along the line of the Ghent-Terneuzen Canal, given the task of clearing an area on the south shore of the Scheldt around the Dutch town of Breskens called the "Breskens pocket". The Polish 1st Armoured Division headed for the Dutch-Belgian border further east and the crucial area north of Antwerp.

The 4th Canadian Armoured advanced from a hard-won bridgehead over the Ghent Canal at Moerbrugge to find themselves the first Allied troops facing the formidable obstacle of the double line of the Leopold and Schipdonk Canals. An attack was mounted in the vicinity of Moerkerke, crossing the canals and establishing a bridgehead before counter-attacks forced a withdrawal with heavy casualties.

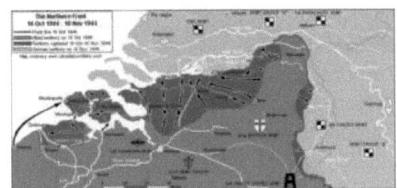

The Northern Front.

The 1st Polish Armoured Division enjoyed greater success to the east as it advanced northeast from Ghent. In country unsuitable for armour, and against stiffening resistance, the Division advanced to the coast by 20 September, occupying Terneuzen and clearing the south bank of the Scheldt east toward Antwerp.

It became apparent to Simonds that any further gains in the Scheldt would come at heavy cost, as the Breskens pocket, extending from Zeebrugge to the Braakman Inlet and inland to the Leopold Canal, was strongly held by the enemy.

Fighting North from Antwerp

On 2 October, the 2nd Canadian Division began its advance north from Antwerp. Stiff fighting at Woensdrecht ensued on 6 October, the objective of the first phase. The Germans—reinforced by Battle Group Chill—saw the priority in holding there, controlling direct access to South Beveland and Walcheren Island.

There were heavy casualties as the Canadians attacked over open, flooded land. Driving rain, booby traps and land mines made advance very difficult. On 13 October 1944, what would come to be known as "Black Friday", the Canadian 5th Infantry Brigade's Black Watch was virtually wiped out in an unsuccessful attack. The Calgary Highlanders were to follow up with a more successful action, and their Carrier Platoon succeeded in taking the rail station at Korteven. Heavy fighting at Hoogerheide also ensued, but by 16 October, Woensdrecht was secured, cutting the land link to South Beveland and Walcheren. The Canadians had achieved their first objective, but suffered heavy casualties.

Member of Canadian Provost Corps talking to members of the Belgian Resistance, Bruges, September 1944.

At this point, recognizing the opportunity, Field-Marshal Bernard Montgomery, issued a directive that made the opening of the Scheldt estuary the top priority of 21st Army Group. To the east, the British Second Army attacked westward to clear the Netherlands south of the Maas River, securing the Scheldt region from counter-attacks.

Meanwhile, Simonds concentrated forces at the neck of the South Beveland peninsula. The 4th Canadian Armoured moved north from the Leopold Canal and took Bergen-op-Zoom. By 24 October, Allied lines were pushed out further from the neck of the peninsula, ensuring German counterattacks wouldn't cut off the 2nd Canadian Division, by then moving west along it towards Walcheren Island.

Operation Switchback

The second main operation of the Battle of the Scheldt opened with fierce fighting to reduce the Breskens pocket. Here, the 3rd Canadian Infantry Division encountered tenacious German resistance as it fought to cross the Leopold Canal.

An earlier failed attempt by the 4th Canadian (Armoured) Division at Moerbrugge had demonstrated the challenge they faced. In addition to the formidable German defences on both the Leopold Canal and the Schipdonk Canal, much of the approach area was flooded.

It was decided that the best place for an assault would be immediately east of where the two canals divided: a narrow strip of dry ground only a few hundred metres wide at its base beyond the Leopold Canal (described as a long triangle with its base on the Maldegem-Aardenburg road and its apex near the village of Moershoofd some five kilometres east).

Members of the 4th Canadian (Armoured) Division demonstrating the use of flame throwers across a canal, Maldegem, October 1944.

A two-pronged assault commenced. The 3rd Canadian Division's 7th Brigade made the initial assault across the Leopold Canal, while the 9th Canadian Infantry Brigade mounted an amphibious attack from the northern or coastal side of the pocket. The assault began on 6 October, supported by extensive artillery and Canadian-built Wasp Universal Carriers, which were equipped with flamethrowers. The Wasps launched their barrage of flame across the Leopold Canal, allowing the 7th Brigade troops to scramble up over the steep banks and launch their assault boats. Two precarious, separate footholds were established, but the enemy recovered from the shock of the flamethrowers and counter-attacked, though they were unable to move the Canadians from their extremely vulnerable bridgeheads. By 9 October, the gap between the bridgeheads was closed, and by early morning on 12 October, a position had been gained across the Aardenburg road.

Corporal Kormendy, a scout from the Calgary Highlanders Scout and Sniper Platoon, in a shot from a series of staged photos by Army photographer Ken Bell, taken near Kapellen, October 1944. PAC Photo

The 9th Canadian Brigade conducted an amphibious operation with the aid of Terrapin (the first such use of this vehicle in Europe) and Buffalo amphibious vehicles, crewed by the British 5th Assault Regiment from the Royal Engineers. The brigade planned to cross the mouth of the Braakman Inlet in amphibious vehicles and to land in the vicinity of Hoofdplaat, a tiny hamlet in the rear or coastal side of the pocket, thus exerting pressure from two directions at once. In spite of difficulties in maneuvering vehicles through the canals and the resulting 24-hour delay, the Germans were taken by surprise and a bridgehead was established. Once again, the Germans recovered quickly and counter-attacked with ferocity; however, they were slowly forced back. The 10th Canadian Brigade, from the 4th Armoured Division, crossed the Leopold Canal and advanced at Isabella Polder. Then the 3rd Division's 8th Canadian Brigade was called to move south from the coastal side of the pocket. This opened up a land-based supply route into the pocket.

The 3rd Division fought additional actions to clear German troops from the towns of Breskens, Oostburg, Zuidzande and Cadzand, as well as the coastal fortress Fort Frederik Hendrik. Operation "Switchback" ended on 3 November, when the First Canadian Army liberated the Belgian towns of Knokke and Zeebrugge, officially closing the Breskens Pocket and eliminating all German forces south of the Scheldt.

Operation Vitality

The third major operation of the Battle of the Scheldt opened on 24 October, when the 2nd Canadian Infantry Division began its advance down the South Beveland peninsula. The Canadians hoped to advance rapidly, bypassing opposition and seizing bridgeheads over the Beveland Canal, but they too were slowed by mines, mud and strong enemy defences.

An amphibious attack was made across the West Scheldt by the British 52nd (Lowland) Division to get in behind the German's Beveland Canal defensive positions. Thus this formidable defence was outflanked, and the Canadian 6th Infantry Brigade began a frontal attack in assault boats. The engineers were able to bridge the canal on the main road.

With the canal line gone, the German defence crumbled and South Beveland was cleared. The third phase of the Battle of the Scheldt was now complete.

Operation Infatuate: Capture of Walcheren Island

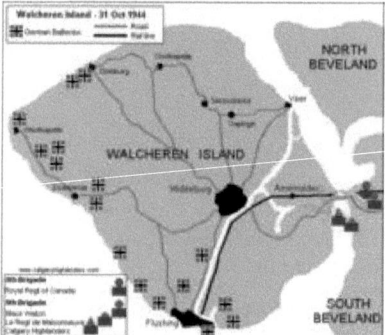

Map of troops at Walcheren Island

Soldiers of the Royal Regiment of Canada rest in Blankenberge, September 1944

As the fourth phase of the Battle of the Scheldt opened, only the island of Walcheren at the mouth of the West Scheldt remained in German hands. The island's defences were extremely strong: heavy coastal batteries on the western and southern coasts defended both the island and the Scheldt estuary, and the coastline had been strongly fortified against amphibious assaults. Furthermore, a landward-facing defensive perimeter had been built around the town of Vlissingen to further defend its port facilities should an Allied landing on Walcheren succeed. The only land approach was the Sloedam—a long, narrow causeway from South Beveland, little more than a raised two-lane road. To make matters more difficult, the flats that surrounded this causeway were too saturated with sea water for movement on foot, but had too little water for an assault in storm boats.

To hamper German defence, the island's dykes were breached by attacks from RAF Bomber Command: on 3 October at Westkapelle, with severe loss of civilian life; on 7 October at two places, west and east of Vlissingen; and on 11 October at Veere. This flooded the central part of the island, forcing the German defenders onto the high ground around the outside and in the towns, but it also allowed the use of amphibious vehicles.

The island was attacked from three directions: across the causeway from the east, across the Scheldt from the south, and by sea from the west.

The Canadian 2nd Infantry Division attacked the causeway on 31 October. An initial attack by the Black Watch was rebuffed; The Calgary Highlanders then sent a company over which was also stopped halfway across the causeway. A second attack by the Highlanders on the morning of 1 November managed to gain a precarious foothold; a day of fighting followed, and then the Highlanders were relieved by Le Regiment de Maisonneuve who struggled to maintain the bridgehead. The "Maisies" withdrew onto the Causeway on 2 November, to be relieved by a battalion of the Glasgow Highlanders of the British 52nd (Lowland) Division. In conjunction with the waterborne attacks, the 52nd continued the advance.

The amphibious landings were conducted in two parts on 1 November. Operation *Infatuate I* consisted mainly of infantry of the British 155th Infantry Brigade (4th and 5th battalions King's Own Scottish Borderers, 7/9th battalion The Royal Scots) and No. 4 Commando, who were ferried across from Breskens in small landing craft to an assault beach in the south-eastern area of Vlissingen, codenamed "Uncle" Beach. During the next few days, they engaged in heavy street fighting against the German defenders.

Operation *Infatuate II* was the amphibious landing at Westkapelle, also conducted on the morning of 1 November. After a heavy naval bombardment by the British Royal Navy, troops of 4th Special Service Brigade (Nos. 41, 47, and 48 Royal Marine Commando and No. 10 Inter Allied Commando, consisting mainly of Belgian and Norwegian troops) supported by specialized armoured vehicles (amphibious transports, mine-clearing tanks, bulldozers, etc.) of the 79th Armoured Division were landed on both sides of the gap in the sea dyke, using large landing craft as well as amphibious vehicles to bring men and tanks ashore. Heavy fighting ensued here as well before the ruins of the town were captured. Part of the troops moved south-eastward, toward Vlissingen, while the main force went north-east to clear the northern half of Walcheren and link up with the Canadian troops who had established a bridgehead on the eastern part of the island. Fierce resistance was again offered by some of the German troops defending this area, so that fighting continued until 7 November.

On 6 November, the island's capital Middelburg fell after a calculated gamble on the Allies' part when the German commander was invited to consider surrendering only to an armoured force. Since Middelburg was impossible to reach with tanks, a force of amphibious Landing Vehicle Tracked ("Buffaloes") were driven into Middelburg, forcing an end to all German resistance on 8 November.

Meanwhile, the 4th Canadian (Armoured) Division had pushed eastward past Bergen-op-Zoom to Sint Philipsland where it sank several German vessels in Zijpe harbor.

With the approaches to Antwerp clear, the fourth phase of the Battle of the Scheldt was complete. The Scheldt was then swept of naval mines, and on 28 November—after much repair of harbor facilities——the first convoy entered the port, led by the Canadian-built freighter *Fort Cataraqui*.

Battle components

From 23 October-5 November 1944, the U.S. 104th Infantry Division experienced its first battle while attached to the British 1st Corps. The division succeeded in pushing through the central portion of North Brabant () against resistance from German snipers and artillery.

Importance of the campaign

At the end of the five-week offensive, the First Canadian Army had taken 41,043 German prisoners. After the first ship arrived on 28 November, convoys started bringing a steady stream of supplies to the continent, which began to reenergize the stalled Allied advance from Paris to the Rhine. Germany recognized the importance of the Allies having a deep water port, so in an attempt to destroy it, or at least disrupt the flow of supplies, the German military fired more V-2 ballistic missiles at Antwerp than any other city. In fact, nearly half of the V-2s launched during the war were fired at Antwerp. The port of Antwerp was so strategically vital, that during the Battle of the Bulge one of the primary German objectives was to retake the city and its port.

Source (edited): "http://en.wikipedia.org/wiki/Battle_of_the_Scheldt"

Belgian Resistance

Belgian resistance during World War II to the occupation of Belgium by Nazi Germany took different forms. "The Belgian Resistance" was the common name for the *Netwerk van de weerstand - Réseau de Résistance* or Resistance Network (RR), a group of partisans fighting the Nazis. Belgian resistance fighters performed various roles, including sabotaging Nazi installations and helping rescue downed Allied fliers. As much of the rail traffic between northern Germany and France passes through Belgium, another role played by networks with radios was to provide the Allies with intelligence on movements of troops and materiel.

Andrée de Jongh organized the Comet Line (*Komeet Lijn - Le Reseau Comète*) for escaped Allied soldiers. Albert Guérisse organized escape routes for downed Allied pilots under the alias of *Patrick Albert "Pat" O'Leary*; his escape line was dubbed the *Pat Line*.

Andree Antoine Dumon helped rescue 27 Allied fliers and worked as a courier for the resistance. Baron Georges Schnek, operating mainly in France and who was Jewish, helped provide false ID papers and ration coupons to fleeing Jewish families.

Georges Schoeters, co-founder and member of the FLQ, worked as a courier towards the end of the war until he was captured by the Nazis.

Background

Belgium was a neutral country but by November 1939 intelligence reports of an impending German attack reached a peak. The Germans had invaded Poland and France had declared war on Germany. The Germans wanted to remove potential aggressors to their west to avoid fighting on two fronts, a strategy which crippled their abilities in World War I. The German Army needed to push through neutral Belgium in order to attack France. The French and British sent soldiers to aid in the fight against the Germans but despite their efforts, the Germans secured the unconditional surrender of Belgium after 18 days of fighting. The King of Belgium, King Leopold III, went against his cabinet by deciding to surrender the country. King Leopold III was taken as a prisoner of war and was later accused by his countrymen of collaborating with the Germans. Despite this, while imprisoned, in 1942 he sent a letter to Adolf Hitler which has been credited with saving an estimated 500,000 Belgian women and children from deportation to munitions factories in Germany. The members of the cabinet retreated to England, where they set up government. Immediately after the surrender, resistance groups were formed to harass the German Army. Due to Germany's failure to sway the Belgian citizens during the German occupation in World War I, the invading army sought to establish itself as a liberating force from British imperialism. However, many citizens were quick to aid in the fight against the Germans. The situation in Belgium is documented in Roger Motz's book *Belgium Unvanquished* in which Motz describes the atmosphere of resistance as being "relentless". Due to the large number of Belgian citizens who were willing to aid the resistance fighters, supply lines were established and evasion routes were charted. The Belgian resistance fighters were determined to aid the Allies in any way they could.

Unusually the Belgian resistance would also come to include the *Légion Belge*, a far right resistance movement led by dissident Rexists who opposed occupation and the National Legion of Paul Hoornaert.

The Independence Front, a mostly communist-led resistance network, was one of the most important in Belgium. It included a specific Austrian communist network, the *Österreichische Freiheitsfront*.

Downed Airmen

The Germans sent out patrols of men with dogs and motorcycles to search for any Allied airman who was shot down. The resistance groups were quick to beat the Germans to the downed flyers. Parachutes needed to be immediately buried and pilots were hidden from the Germans. The Comet Line had a series of safe houses throughout Belgium. Allied airmen were given civilian clothes and frequently moved from house to house, staying with Belgian families who supported the resistance. The resistance would aid the airmen by giving them false papers and guiding them to either neutral or Allied occupied territory. German soldiers would fail to recognize that some of the men passing through their checkpoints were actually allied pilots who were being transported out of Belgium. One incident was captured on film where a German soldier was shown lighting the cigarette of an American Navigator who was disguised as a Belgian civilian. Though many airmen were able to escape successfully, many others were caught by the Germans, sometimes after months of successful evasion. Captured airmen were interrogated by the Gestapo before being imprisoned in Belgium or transported back to German POW camps.

Bridge over the Ambleve River

German troops were moved by train from stations in Belgium. The resistance network monitored these transport trains to determine the patterns of German troop movement. Herman Bodson was a Belgian chemist before the war broke out in Europe. Bodson was heavily involved with the Comet line and worked with allied Special Forces during the war. He also served as a medic during the Battle of the Bulge He worked with several resistance units in and around Brussels. Allied commanders passed on targets to the men, who would carry out the sabotage missions. Bodson had received reports that the German Army was constantly sending trains full of German soldiers throughout Belgium. The resistance network quickly identified when and where troop trains would be traveling. The plan was to destroy a vital bridge between the towns of La Gleize and Stoumont. A group of nearly 40 members of the Belgian Resistance assembled at the bridge and quickly began placing explosives on the bridge's center arch. As a German troop train approached the bridge, the explosives were detonated. The train, unable to stop in time, crashed into the river killing all 600 German soldiers aboard. Belgian saboteurs received much of their supplies, including explosives and arms by stealing them from German munitions dumps and during skirmishes with the German Army. One faction of the resistance, known as *Group G* carried out numerous successful sabotage missions. The Germans were continuously tested by the resistance groups. Throughout the war *Group G* caused the Germans to expend 20 million man-hours of labor to repair damages done by the underground.

Casualties

Resistance fighters were constantly working to overthrow the occupying Germans. Their missions often went unseen but any resistance fighters captured by the Germans would either be imprisoned or shot. Losses were felt hard in the resistance community. Members were always at risk of being captured or betrayed. The Germans had special agents working against the resistance forces. The agents were told to make connections within the underground communities in order to gather intelligence. Escape routes were sometimes traps and many downed airmen, as well as resistance fighters, were captured this way. German soldiers, working within the resistance groups were responsible for the arrests of hundreds of Belgian citizens, Allied soldiers and resistance fighters.

Achievements

One of the objectives of the resistance was to provide an evasion route for Allied pilots who had been shot down over areas occupied by the Germans. Many of the resistance fighters sought to harass the German Army into withdrawing from Belgian territories.

Resistance fighters were also credited with stopping a train which was transporting Jewish prisoners to Auschwitz. This train was labeled the Twentieth convoy.

The use of sabotage as an effective weapon was not heavily utilized until World War II. The German Army lost thousands of trains during the war due to acts of sabotage. German units were spread throughout Europe and many smaller units were targeted by resistance fighters. Ambushes were a common tactic used. Rail lines were very often targeted to disrupt the flow of materials and men for the German Army. Stretches of track were rigged with explosive charges and would be set to explode as the train passes over them. The resistance groups costs the German Army millions of dollars worth of equipment and had a large psychological effect on the German soldiers. By stalling and delaying the German forces, the Belgian Resistance group prevented the Axis from ever establishing a stable base of operations in occupied Belgium.

Popular culture

- A 1977 film, *Secret Agents*, dealt with the Belgian Resistance.
- A BBC series, Secret Army, was filmed during the late 1970s based on Comète Line
- An American documentary in 2006 called "Last Best Hope" premiered in Brussels for Prince Phillipe, the Belgian Army, and diplomats from five countries. Film makers David Grosvenor, Mat Hames, Ramona Kelly, and Walter Verstraeten presented the film to surviving Belgian Resistance members Andrée de Jongh, Raymond Itterbeek, Michou and Nadine Dumon and others. An edited version aired in the U.S. on PBS in 2006 and 2007 and on European television in 2007.
- A History Channel documentary called Nazi Ghost Train was released in 2000 and interviews members of the Belgian Resistance at a reunion. Surviving Allied pilots also attend to pay respect to the men and women who risked their lives to keep them from falling into German hands.

Source (edited): "http://en.wikipedia.org/wiki/Belgian_Resistance"

Comet line

The **Comet line** *(Le Réseau Comète)* was a World War II resistance group in Belgium/France which helped Allied soldiers and airmen return to Britain. The line started in Brussels, where the men were fed, clothed and given false identity papers before being hidden in attics and cellars of houses. A network of people guided them south through occupied France into neutral Spain and home via British-controlled Gibraltar.

Routes

A typical route was from Brussels or Lille to Paris and then via Tours, Bordeaux, Bayonne, over the Pyrenees to San Sebastián in Spain. From there evaders travelled to Bilbao, Madrid and Gibraltar. There were three other main routes. The Pat line (after founder Pat O'Leary) ran from Paris to Toulouse via Limoges and then over the Pyrenees via Esterri d'Aneu to Barcelona. Another Pat line ran from Paris to Dijon, Lyons, Avignon to Marseille, then Nîmes, Perpignan and Barcelona. From Barcelona evaders were transported to Gibraltar.

Another route from Paris (the Shelburne line) ran to Rennes and then St Brieuc in Brittany, where men were shipped to Dartmouth.

Creation and exploits

The Comet line was created by a young Belgian woman who joined the Belgian Resistance. Andrée de Jongh (nickname "Dédée") was 24 in 1940 and lived in Brussels. She was the younger daughter of Frédéric de Jongh, a headmaster, and Alice Decarpentrie. Edith Cavell, a British nurse shot in the Tir National in Schaerbeek in 1915 for assisting troops to escape from occupied Belgium to the neutral Netherlands, had been a heroine of Dédée's in her youth.

In August 1941, Andrée de Jongh appeared in the British consulate in Bilbao with a British soldier, James Cromar from Aberdeen, and two Belgian volunteers, Merchiers and Sterckmans, having travelled by train through Paris to Bayonne and then on foot over the Pyrenees. She requested support for her escape network (later named Comet line) from the British military intelligence, granted by MI9, (British Military Intelligence Section 9), under the control of an ex-infantry major, Norman Crockatt and escaped Colditz Castle POW lieutenant Airey Neave.

With MI9 she helped 400 Allied soldiers escape from Belgium through occupied France to the British consulate in Madrid and on to Gibraltar. Neave described her as "one of our greatest agents." Later Neave organised gunboats from Dartmouth, Devon, to cross the Channel and run agents and supplies to the French resistance in Brittany and to return escaped POWs and evaders to Britain.

Comet Line members and the families took great risks, De Jongh escorting 118 airmen over the Pyrenees herself.

After November 1942 escape lines became more dangerous when southern France was occupied by the Germans and the whole of France was under Nazi rule. Many members of the Comet line were betrayed, hundreds were arrested by the Geheime Feldpolizei and the Abwehr and after weeks of interrogation and torture at places such as Fresnes Prison in Paris were executed or labelled Nacht und Nebel (NN) prisoners. NN prisoners were deported to German prisons and many later to concentration camps such as Ravensbrück concentration camp for women, Mauthausen-Gusen concentration camp, Buchenwald concentration camp, Flossenbürg concentration camp,

Prisoners sent to these camps included Andrée de Jongh, Elsie Maréchal (Belgian Resistance), Nadine Dumon (Belgian Resistance), Mary Lindell (Comtesse de Milleville) and Virginia d'Albert-Lake (American).

The authors of the official history of MI9 cite 2,373 British and Commonwealth servicemen and 2,700 Americans taken to Britain during World War II. The RAF Escaping Society estimated there were 14,000 helpers officially in 1945. The Comet line inspired the 1970s BBC television series, *Secret Army* (1977–79).

Notable members of the Line

- Andrée de Jongh, (aka Dédée) Line creator and chief. Arrested 15 January 1943. Survived several Nazi concentration camps. Awarded the George Medal
- Frédéric de Jongh, (aka Paul). Dédée's father. Arrested 7 June 1943. Executed 28 March 1944.
- Baron Jean Greindl, (aka Nemo). Head of line in Brussels. Arrested 6 February 1943. Killed 7 September 1943.
- Elvire de Greef, (aka Tante Go). Organiser in South France. Escaped arrest and survived. Awarded the George Medal
- Jean-François Nothomb, (aka Franco). Succeeded Dedee in France. Arrested 18 January 1944. Survived several Nazi concentration camps. Awarded the Distinguished Service Order.
- Comte Jacques Legrelle (aka Jerome), organised and operated line in the Paris area, linked theBelgium part of line to South of France. Was captured, tortured, sent to concentration camps and survived. Awarded the George Medal.
- Comte Antoine d'Ursel (aka Jacques Cartier). Succeeded Nemo in Brussels. Died crossing Franco-Spanish border 24 December 1943.
- Micheline Dumon (aka Michou), Operated line in 1944. Escaped arrest and awarded the George Medal.

Source (edited): "http://en.wikipedia.org/wiki/Comet_line"

Comité de Défense des Juifs

The ***Comité de Défense des Juifs*** (*CDJ*, Dutch: *Joods Verdedigingscomiteit, JVD*, Jews' defense committee) was an organization of the Belgian Resistance, affiliated to the *Front de l'Indépendance*, founded by the Jewish Communist Hertz Jospa and his wife Have Groisman (Yvonne Jospa) of the Jewish Revolutionary organization *Solidarité juive* in September 1942.

The *CDJ* had thirty-odd members in its children's section alone. These members formed an effective committee and came from all political and religious horizons, overcoming their divergent views to unite for the sake of saving Jewish children. The *CDJ* succeeded in saving about 3,500 of the 5,000 children who became *enfants cachés* ("hidden children", hidden among non-Jewish Belgian families, convents, etc.). The *CDJ* was also involved in other aspects of the resistance, producing the clandestine publications such as *Unser Kampf* ("Our Battle").

The *CDJ* also functioned as a national organisation in the field of social services. The section Kinderen (Children) became responsible for hiding and supporting those who had gone underground. The co-operation and assistance from the non-Jewish sector was remarkable. Thanks to 'unarmed resistance fighters' more than 3,000 Jews were rescued from deportation. The price paid for this campaign, however, was high. Many members of the *CDJ* together with their fellow collaborators were arrested by the authorities.

Source (edited): "http://en.wikipedia.org/wiki/Comit%C3%A9_de_D%C3%A9fense_des_Juifs"

Free Belgian Forces

The **Free Belgian Forces** were members of the Belgian armed forces in World War II who continued fighting against the Axis after the surrender of Belgium and its subsequent occupation by the Germans. The Belgians fought in several theaters of the war, including Great Britain, East Africa, the Mediterranean, and Northwestern Europe.

The decision of King Léopold III to surrender on May 28, 1940 was not accepted by members of the Belgian government-in-exile (under Prime-Minister Hubert Pierlot), who had fled first to Paris and later to London. Under the auspices of this government, Belgian armed forces were organized to continue military operations as part of the Allies, and existing Belgian colonial troops in the Belgian Congo were made available to the Allied war effort.

Free Belgian Forces: Army

The ground troops of the Free Belgian Forces were drawn from three main sources during the course of the war. These were the Force Publique in the Congo, expatriate Belgians in Great Britain and Canada, and after September 1944, Belgians liberated by the Allied campaign in Northwestern Europe.

The *Force Publique* in Africa

Three brigades of infantry were mobilized from the "Public Force" (*Force Publique*) in the Belgian Congo to fight with the Allies in Africa. In 1940 and 1941, the "Belgian Expeditionary Forces" fought in the British and Commonwealth campaign to defeat the Italian troops in East Africa (East African Campaign). In late May 1941, Belgian Major-General Auguste-Éduard Gilliaert cut off the retreat of Italian General Pietro Gazzera in Ethiopia and accepted the surrender of 7,000 of his troops.

After the successful conclusion of these campaigns, the 1st Belgian Colonial Brigade was redesignated the Belgian Colonial Motor Brigade Group and served in a garrison and rear-area security role in Cairo, Egypt and in British Palestine during 1943 - 1944.

The Force Publique had older weapons and equipment such as the Stokes Mortar and the St Chamond 75 mm gun.

The Force Publique also sent the 10th Belgian Congo Casualty Clearing Station (CCCS) to the battle zone. Between 1940 and 1945 some 350 Congolese and twenty Belgians, under the command of Medical Colonel Thomas, worked together with the British medical services in Abyssinia, Somalia, Madagascar and Burma.

Brigade Piron

Memorial to the Belgian Commandos in Ostend, Belgium.

Belgians and some Luxembourgers in Great Britain and Canada, including 163 rescued from Dunkirk, were recruited from May 25, 1940 to form the 1st Belgian Infantry Brigade. The commander of the Belgian ground troops in Great Britain was Lieutenant General van Strydonck de Burkel. Because of the shortage of Belgian manpower, the unit grew slowly, first formed as a battalion, and finally as a brigade in January 1943. Initially, for operations in northwestern Europe, the brigade had three motorized rifle companies, an artillery battery (of which one troop (four guns) was Luxembourgian), an engineer company, an armored car squadron, and combat support units. The brigade landed at Arromanches in Normandy on August 8, 1944 and fought for the next month on the Normandy coast of France, within the 1st Canadian Army. It was reassigned to the 2nd British Army at short notice and moved to Belgium on September 3 and this allowed the Brigade to assist the liberation of its home country and southern Netherlands. In November 1944, it returned to Belgium and reorganized. The reorganized brigade had three infantry battalions, an artillery regiment of six batteries, and an armored car regiment. Returning to combat in the Netherlands in April 1945, the brigade's units fought at Nijmegen and Walcheren. Also known as *Brigade Piron* (for its commander, Colonel Jean Piron), the Belgian Brigade was equipped with British weapons and material.

Belgian Special Forces

Belgian soldiers in Great Britain also contributed a troop (company) to the British commandos (assigned as 4 Troop, No. 10 Inter-Allied Commando). The Belgian commandos fought in Norway, France, Madagascar, Italy, Yugoslavia, on Walcheren, and in Germany. In late 1944, two other troops of commandos were formed from liberated manpower who had been members of the Belgian resistance. Belgium also contributed a battalion-sized regiment to the Special Air Service, fighting in northern France, occupied Belgium, and the Netherlands during 1944 - 1945.

The Fusilier Battalions

Memorial to the 11th Fusilier Battalion, located in Namur.

Liberated manpower was used to form 57 fusilier (infantry) battalions, four engineer and four pioneer battalions, and 34 motor transport battalions from October 1944 until June 1945. The bulk of the Fusilier battalions were used to secure rear areas. This task grew demanding as large areas of Germany were overrun in 1945 and the presence of the lightly equipped Belgian units allowed better equipped units of the major allies to pursue combat operations and not have to detach elements for security of their lines of communication. However, some 20 of the Fusilier battalions were used in combat in the Ardennes Offensive, in the Netherlands, at the Remagen Bridgehead, and in Czechoslovakia at Pilsen. Among Belgians today, the 5th Fusilier Battalion is particularly remembered for its service with the U.S. Army during the Ardennes Offensive.

In the Far East

The Belgian 10th Casualty Clearing Station supported operations in Burma and Indonesia.

Free Belgian Forces: Navy

During the war, the Belgian Navy operated two corvettes and a group of minesweepers. The Navy participated in the Battle of the Atlantic, and had 350 men by May 1943.

Free Belgian Forces: Air Force

The initial Belgian fliers with the Royal Air Force were individual members of British squadrons. Belgium contributed 29 pilots to Fighter Command during the Battle of Britain. Although usually randomly posted to various RAF fighter squadrons, No. 609 Squadron had enough Belgian pilots to form a flight. Later, some of the Belgian pilots were organized into two all-Belgian squadrons, the No. 350 (Belgian) Squadron (formed November 1941) and No. 349 (Belgian) Squadron (formed November 1942). By June 1943, some 400 Belgian pilots were serving with the RAF. Initially part of the air defense of Great Britain, both squadrons later served in the campaign in northwestern Europe supporting 21st Army Group with No. 83 and No. 84 Groups of the R.A.F. The British air raid on Gestapo headquarters in Copenhagen on March 22, 1945 was led by a Belgian Wing Commander, Michael Donnet. Altogether, some 1,200 Belgians served in the R.A.F. The Belgian Squadrons flew Spitfires operationally with the RAF. No. 350 Squadron claimed some 51 kills during its existence.

Postwar

Ultimately, Belgium mobilized some 100,000 men under arms between the time Belgium surrendered in 1940 and VE Day in 1945. After the war, five of the brigades mobilized by Belgium with liberated manpower and the Brigade Piron formed two divisions of the new Belgian Army and were used in the occupation of Germany. The Belgian commandos and S.A.S. troops were ultimately used to form the Belgian Paracommando Regiment, and 349 and 350 Squadrons of the RAF formed the postwar Belgian Air Force.
Source (edited): "http://en.wikipedia.org/wiki/Free_Belgian_Forces"

Front de l'Indépendance

The *Front de l'indépendance* (FI) (Independence Front, in Dutch: *Onafhankelijkheidsfront* – OF) was a Belgian resistance movement during World War II, founded in March 1941 by Dr. Albert Marteaux of the Communist Party of Belgium, Father André Roland, and Fernand Demany, another communist. The aim of the organisation was to unite Belgian resistance groups of all opinions and political leanings; nonetheless the only political party that that was affiliated as such was the Belgian communist party.

By the end of the war, the *Front de l'indépendance* contained representatives from a large number of organisations, including:
- The *Partisans armés* (PA, armed partisans),
- The *Milices patriotiques* (MP, patriotic milita),
- *Solidarité* (Solidarity, founded in 1942 as the social service of the F.I. to help victims of the Nazi repression and their families, those who refused to go in Germany under the Service du travail obligatoire, foreign illegals etc.; the Belgian section of the Secours Rouge continued within this clandestine organization),
- The *Comités de lutte syndicale* (Unions' committee for the struggle)
- *Wallonie Libre* (Free Wallonia),
- The *Comité de Défense des Juifs* (Jews' defense committee)
- LOMO (Dutch: *Leraren Officieel Middelbaar Onderwijs*, Middle school teachers of the public network in Flanders), whose leader Aloïs Gerlo (1915-1998) was an activist of the Communist Party between 1940 and 1956
- *Front*, the underground newspaper
- The *Österreichische Freiheitsfront*, an antifascist organisation created in Brussels by communist refugees from Austria and Germany.

Through these various organisations, the *Front de l'indépendance* established sabotage operations, escape routes and a false document service, and distributed 250 different underground publications. This essential part of the war, in the area of information, found a culmination of sorts in the publication by the *Front* on 9 November 1943 of *Faux Soir*, a spoof version of the *Le Soir* newspaper circulated under the noses of the occupation authorities.

In February 1943, the *Front de l'indépendance* sent the sociologist Victor Martin on a spying mission in Germany to search for reliable information about what happened to the Jews deported to Germany. He came back in May with the first reliable report on their fate, as well as with detailed information on the functioning of the Auschwitz concentration camp.
Source (edited): "http://en.wikipedia.org/wiki/Front_de_l%27Ind%C3%A9pendance"

Nazi Ghost Train

The **Nazi Ghost Train** was a train used by the Gestapo in 1944 to transport Belgian prisoners and Allied airmen into Germany. It's mission was thwarted by the underground organization known as the "Comet Line" with the help of the Belgian Resistance who managed to stop the train from reaching concentration camps in Germany with the prisoners. Through several acts of sabotage, they made sure the train never got very far out of Brussels into the hands of the Germans.

Background

With the Germans occupying most of western Europe during World War II, the lives of allied soldiers and airmen became an issue, inspiring the creation of the Comet Line. The Comet Line was an organization dedicated to helping allied military personnel, with the Belgian resistance hard at work. Because they were able to stop the train, it is considered part of the Belgian resistance movement.

The rising dangers the Belgian resistance workers had due to the increased German scrutiny made safe train crossings in July 1943 through the rest of the country very difficult, forcing the Comet Line to find alternate routes. Unfortunately, finding alternate routes became an even bigger difficulty. The headquarters in Paris, where most of the Comet Line's escape lines were located, had just been discovered by the Germans in January 1944, making even Paris unsafe for some of the Belgians. Including the invasion of the headquarters by the Germans, Belgian ranks of Comet became thin because the Germans captured a few resistance groups and leaders, one of which being Jean Masson, making the beginning of 1944 in Paris terrible. Masson, a Belgian from Tourcoing who had recently began working in the line, was later discovered to have worked for the Paris Gestapo. He started work again in early January 1944.

Description of train

The train itself was a line of 20 cattle cars formed by the Germans at Brussels' south rail station in Brussels, known as Gare du Midi. It was filled with scote Saint Gilles prisoners and 54 airmen on their way to Germany, who previously had been arrested in safe houses waiting to be moved to Luflagers.

Acts of sabotage

When the train headed off on 1 September 1944 for Germany, the departure of the train was delayed by rail employees and engine problems, but the main cause to the thwarted journey to the concentration camps was due to the Belgian resistance sabotages. These sabotages included tracks being blown up, a sabotaged water supply, and an engineer deliberately throwing himself off the train, therefore halting the journey due to the loss of a driver. The next day, the train returned to Brussels Grande Ile Station to find that Brussels had been liberated by the British. At that moment, the doors of the train were forced open, releasing civilian prisoners first, following the 54 airmen. The airmen disappeared joyously into the celebrating city, finally free from the Germans. Their jobs were to contact British forces in town to learn where they report to next: the British temporary headquarters at the Hotel Metropole in Brussels. They then received temporary uniforms, following an evacuation to a lorry convoy toward Lille, France.

Aftermath

Because of the resistance's remarkable acts of courage, the train never reached its destination, saving thousands of lives. 776 victims were helped, and 288 were passed into Spain by nearly one thousand Belgian and French helpers from the Comet Line. About 800 of those helpers were later arrested for their risky actions.

Television productions

The story of the Nazi Ghost Train was recently turned into a short documentary produced by the History Channel in its series History's Mysteries in 2000. The Nazi Ghost Train includes survivors that recount the astonishing tale of heroism under fire, where scores of people risked their lives to save souls bound for the Nazi death machine.
Source (edited): "http://en.wikipedia.org/wiki/Nazi_Ghost_Train"

Robert Jan Verbelen

Robert Jan Verbelen (April 5, 1911, Herent, Belgium – c. September 1990) was a Belgian Nazi collaborator. After the liberation of Belgium in the Second World War, Verbelen fled through Germany to Austria, where for eight years he worked for the Counter Intelligence Corps of the US Army, while he already was convicted as war criminal in Belgium. He obtained Austrian citizenship in 1959. He was charged with five murders in a 1965 war crime trial in Austria, but was acquitted of war crimes.

During the last years of the War, Verbelen was head of the *De Vlag Veiligheidscorps*, a Nazi SS security force in Belgium. In that function he assassinated Alexandre Galopin, director of the Société Générale de Belgique, and tried to murder Albert Devèze, Minister of State, Charles Collard-de Sloovere, Attorney General, and Robert de Foy, former State Security director. He was sentenced to the death penalty by a Belgian court in 1947, who found him responsible for the deaths of 101 Belgian resistance fighters.

Source (edited): "http://en.wikipedia.org/wiki/Robert_Jan_Verbelen"

Todor Angelov

Todor Angelov Dzekov (Bulgarian: Тодор Ангелов Дзеков, French: *Théodore Angheloff*; Kyustendil 12 January 1900 – Fort Breendonk 30 November 1943) was a Bulgarian communist revolutionary who lived and was active for a long time in Western Europe. During World War II, he headed a Brussels-based group of the Belgian Resistance against Nazi Germany; he was captured and sentenced to death by the Nazis.

Angelov was born in 1900 in the city of Kyustendil to a mason father and a weaver and laundress mother, both Bulgarian refugees from Macedonia. In 1923 he married Aleksandra Sharlandzhieva; the two had a daughter, the writer Svoboda Bachvarova (b. 1925). Angelov was related to the anarchist left wing of Internal Macedonian Revolutionary Organization (IMRO) and the Bulgarian Communist Party from an early age; in 1923 he took part in the failed and suppressed September Uprising, more specifically in its Pirin Macedonia operations. After the communist St Nedelya Church assault of 1925, he was sentenced to death but managed to escape the country with his family.

After spending some time in Austria and France, Angelov and his family settled in Belgium in 1927. In 1930 they were extradited for "disturbing public peace": Angelov settled in Luxembourg while his wife and daughter returned to Bulgaria. In 1932 he was allowed to return to Belgium. In 1936–1938, he joined the International Brigades' Dimitrov Battalion of Bulgarian volunteers and fought in the Spanish Civil War, siding with the Second Spanish Republic forces.

Upon returning to Belgium Angelov was an active supporter of the Communist Party of Belgium. In 1942, he organized a resistance group of around 25 people, mostly Central Europeean Jewish immigrants; the group was mostly active around Brussels. Angelov was referred to as *Terrorist X* by the Nazi authorities and led over 200 actions against the Nazis, including the destruction of a train carrying military machinery and the burning of records of Jews to be deported. During a single year, around half of the group's members were killed or arrested. Angelov was arrested in early 1943 and interned in the Fort Breendonk concentration camp, where he was executed in late November the same year.

Immediately following the war, Angelov was proclaimed a hero of Belgian Resistance and awarded a posthumous Order of Leopold. In the early 1980s, a monument to him was built in the Clos du Chemin creux in Schaerbeek, where he lived for a long time. A monument to Angelov also exists in his hometown Kyustendil; he was proclaimed a honorary citizen of Kyustendil in 1998.

In 2007, the book *Otages de la terreur nazie* ("Hostages of Nazi Terror") devoted to Angelov and his group was issued in Belgium. In 2008, the Bulgarian writer Svoboda Bachvarova published the three-volume documentary novel *Po osobeno machitelen nachin* ("In a Particularly Painful Way") devoted to her father's life.

Source (edited): "http://en.wikipedia.org/wiki/Todor_Angelov"

Twentieth convoy

The 2nd statue created to remember the resistance action against the 20th Jew transport in Belgium. Location: railway station Boortmeerbeek, Belgium. Date picture: 29.08.2005.

Date picture: 29.08.2005.

Transport 20 (XXth convoy) was a Jewish prisoner transport in Belgium organized by the Nazi Germany during World War II. Members of the Belgian Resistance freed Jewish and Gypsy civilians who were being transported by train from the Dossin Barracks located in Mechelen, Belgium to the Auschwitz concentration camp. This rescue of Jews being transported was unique in the European history of the Holocaust.

Background

In 1940, nearly 70,000 Jews were living in Belgium. Of these, 46 percent were deported from the former Dossin army base in Mechelen, while a further 5,034 people were deported via the Drancy internment camp (close to Paris). The Reichssicherheitshauptamt (RSHA) in Berlin was responsible for organizing the transport and the chief of the Dossin Barracks (sammellager) prepared the paper convoy list in triplicate. One copy was for the police officer in charge of security during the transport, the second for the *sammellager* in Mechelen and the third for the BSD-department located in Brussels. Because all the copies for the Dossin Barracks were preserved, historians have been able to trace and map all the German transports of Belgian Jews to the concentration camps. From the summer of 1942 until 1944, twenty-eight transports left Belgium to bring 25,257 Jews and 351 Roma (gypsies) to eastern Europe. Their destination was often Auschwitz. On April 19, 1943, the twentieth transport left with 1631 Jewish men, women and children, heading for Germany. For the first time the 3rd class wagons were replaced by freight wagons with barbed wire covering the small windows. Also, a special wagon, Sonderwagen, was added with 19 Jews (18 men and one women) consisting of resistance members and "jumpers" from previous Transports. These "special list" prisoners were marked in the back of their clothes with a cross painted in red, in order to kill them immediately on arrival at Auschwitz. Eventually, three prisoners escaped from the wagon, a fourth was shot.

The rescue

Three young students and members of the Belgian resistance a Jewish doctor, Youra Livschitz and his two non-Jewish friends Robert Maistriau and Jean Franklemon, armed with one pistol, a lantern and red paper to create a makeshift red lantern (to use as a danger signal), were able to stop the train on the track Mechelen-Leuven, between the municipalities of Boortmeerbeek and Haacht. The twentieth convoy was guarded by one officer and fifteen men from the Sicherheitspolizei, who came from Germany. Despite this security measure, Maistriau was able to open one wagon and liberate 17 people. Many other escaped from the convoy without any connection with the attack. In all, 231 people escaped: 90 Jews who were recaptured and put on another convoy, 26 others who were killed, and 115 who succeeded in escaping. The youngest (Simon Gronowski) was only 11 years old. Regine Krochmal, an eighteen-year-old nurse with the resistance, also escaped after she cut the wooden bars put in front of the train air inlet with a breadknife and jumped from the train near Haacht. Both survived World War II.

Direction Auschwitz

On April 22, 1943, the train arrived at Auschwitz. During the selection, only 521 ID numbers are assigned. Of these 521, only 150 people survived the war. The remaining 1,031 people disappeared in the Holocaust. Based on a telegram dated April 29, 1943 from Reichssicherheitshauptamt to E. Ehlers, SS-Obersturmbannführer and Chief of the Belgian Sicherheitspolizei (Sipo-SD), historians assume that at the time of the arrival of the twentieth convoy at Auschwitz, some problems existed. The rumours of the *Endlösung* created some revolt against the Germans.

Aftermath

The twentieth convoy was an exceptionally large convoy and was the first transport to use freight cars with doors fenced with barbed-wire. The previous transports used 3rd class wagons on which it was easy to escape through the windows. After the twentieth convoy, each convoy was reinforced with a German reserve company (based in Brussels) until it reached the German border.

In remembrance of the action of the

resistance, a statue was inaugurated in 1993 near the train station of Boortmeerbeek. It remembers the Holocaust and the transport of 25,257 Jews, (including 5,093 children) and 352 Roma over the railway track Mechelen-Leuven to the concentration camps. Only 1,205 persons returned home alive.

Source (edited): "http://en.wikipedia.org/wiki/Twentieth_convoy"

Wallonie Libre

Rattachist Flag

Wallonie Libre or **Free Wallonia** is a small political movement in Belgium. It is believed to have been founded on June 18, 1940 on the battlegrounds of Waterloo in the Brabant province, the place where Napoleon was defeated in 1815 by the British, Prussian and Russian armies. Wallingants, the Walloon nationalists, used this battleground in the Interbellum for the purpose of propaganda and demonstrations. Free Wallonia claims to be the eldest resistance movement against nazism in Belgium.

Throughout history, the Free Wallonia movement has been known by far as the only true Wallingant organization in Belgium. It organised the so-called *combat wallon*, the Walloon combat, leading to the 1980 Congress where the movement began to call for complete Walloon independence. Notable moments in their history were the riots in 1950 following the Royal Question, the organization of an annual National Walloon Congress and the 1960-1961 Winter General Strike, following the adoption of the Unique Law.

In 2005, Jacques Rogissart, the then national leader of Free Wallonia, decided to join the Rassemblement Wallonie-France (*Rally Wallonia-France*), led by Paul-Henry Gendebien. He created a counter-organization called **Nouvelle Wallonie Libre** (*New Free Wallonia*). He was replaced by Jacques Dupont.

Source (edited): "http://en.wikipedia.org/wiki/Wallonie_Libre"

William Herskovic

William Herskovic

William Herskovic (June 1914 - March 3, 2006) was a Holocaust survivor and humanitarian. His escape from Auschwitz in 1942 and early eyewitness testimony inspired Belgium's opposition to Nazi Germany during World War II, and alerted the Resistance to the atrocities that were taking place in the concentration camps. Because of Herskovic's escape and testimony, hundreds of lives were saved.

Herskovic is also the founder of Bel Air Camera, a veritable landmark in Los Angeles, which he established in 1957, and has received numerable awards for his philanthropy.

Early life
Herskovic was born in June 1914 in what was then Hungary.

His mother died when he was only 6 months old, and his father had many children by a second wife, so he was raised mainly by his maternal grandparents.

Herskovic, who spoke 9 languages, dropped out of school at the age of 13 in order to take his brother's place as a photographer's apprentice. By the age of 15 he was running photo studios across Czechoslovakia and winning awards as an artist for his skill in photographic retouching.

By the age of 17, he had started his own photo studio, Studio Willy, that quickly gained fame across Belgium.

He married his first wife, Esther, and they had two girls—Giselle (Katie) Herskovic, born in 1938, and Germaine Herskovic, born in 1941.

Holocaust experiences
Herskovic's businesses were confiscated by the Germans and he, his wife and their two baby girls were sent to a concentration camp. All though he wouldn't find out until a long time later, his wife and two daughters were killed in a gas chamber almost immediately upon their arrival.

Herskovic was sent to an Auschwitz hard labor camp where he wasn't expected to live long on about 130 calories a day.

Herskovic set about planning an escape, and on the first night of Hanukkah, 1942, Herskovic and two others dug a pair of wire cutters out from beneath layers of snow where they had hidden them, and cut through chain-link fences during a blizzard.

The three ran through the snow for hours towards freedom.

Herskovic then warned the Belgian underground of what was going on in the camps. "Do not go peacefully, they are killing us by the hundreds," he is quoted as saying in *Escape to Life: A Journey Through the Holocaust*, his biography.

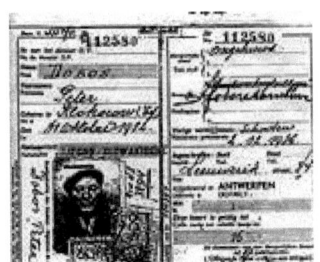

Herskovic's forged "Peter Dobos" identity papers

The resistance quickly mobilized, stopping a transport train and rescuing hundreds bound for the camps.

"His survival saved hundreds," according to a Simon Wiesenthal Center tribute.

Herskovic then went undercover, carefully crafting false papers and getting a job camouflaging the beaches of Normandy, where he was in fact observing military installations and drawing sketches to send back to the resistance.

After the war

Herskovic, discovering that his wife and children had been killed, asked his first wife's younger sister, Maria, for her hand in marriage (her husband had also been killed in the Holocaust). She accepted.

They had three children, all girls, and moved to America. In Los Angeles, Herskovic founded Bel Air Camera in 1957 in Westwood Village, which is still a family-owned business to this day.

From the moment he immigrated to the U.S. with his wife, Mireille, they began their heartfelt dedication to philanthropy, contributing to communities whenever possible. With an understandable commitment to his history, he was a founding supporter of the U.S. Holocaust Museum in Washington, D.C. where a plaque proudly commemorates, and hopefully puts to rest, all the beloved family he lost who were never given the benefit of gravestones. He was also dedicated to the Simon Wiesenthal Museum of Tolerance in hopes, "that education and awareness will prevent prejudice and hatred in the future." Additionally, he and his wife have been loyal supporters of numerous organizations including: UJF, ADL, Friends of Sheba Medical Center, Friends of Israel Disabled Veterans, Technion, UCLA's Hillel, Milken Community High School, Stephen S. Wise Temple, The Jesters (a charity helping blind children), Israel Cancer Research Fund, and others.

Awards

Throughout his life, Herskovic received numerous awards for his heroic and philanthropic work. Most recently, he was given the Humanitarian Award by the Israel Cancer Research Fund.

Death

William Herskovic died on March 3, 2006 at his home in Encino, CA after a long battle with prostate cancer. He was 91. Herskovic is survived by his wife, Maria, their three children, four grandchildren and great-grandchild.

Source (edited): "http://en.wikipedia.org/wiki/William_Herskovic"

Österreichische Freiheitsfront

The *Österreichische Freiheitsfront* (Austrian Freedom Front) was an antifascist organization created by Austrian and German communist refugees in Brussels during the Second World War occupation of Belgium by Nazi Germany. It took an active part in the Belgian Resistance.

History

Allied to the Front de l'Indépendance, a resistance network with a strong communist component, the main mission of the *Österreichische Freiheitsfront* was publishing and spreading leaflets in German. Among these was the periodical *Die Wahrheit* (The Truth), which contained messages from the British and Free Polish radios, inciting the German soldiers to desert.

A member of the organization, Régine Krochmal, explained that the approaching technique was to ask a soldier for time in German, then begin to chat with him. If he was found open to criticism of the Nazi régime, an appointment was fixed in order to give him leaflets to spread. Such an act could lead to the death penalty for those caught.

According to another survivor, Jakob Zanger, the weekly circulation of *Die Wahrheit*, *Österreichische Freiheitsfront*, and from 1943 *Freies Österreich* surpassed 12,000, of which 9,000 were distributed outside Brussels. Copies were left in airports, movie theaters and other places frequented by German soldiers, to ensure a maximal circulation. The newspaper of the Austrian Communist Party, *Rote Fahne* (Red Flag), was clandestinely printed in Belgium on cigarette paper and transported to Austria.

Among the members of the *Österreichische Freiheitsfront* was Jean Améry (pseudonym of Hans Mayer, 1912–1978), an Austrian Catholic writer of Jewish origin. He was arrested in 1943 and deported to Auschwitz-Monowitz.

Toward the end of 1943 or beginning of 1944, a company of Austrian partisans was created, under the aegis of which Erich Ungar, a teacher and physical chemist, made bombs and explosives. Arms and munitions were obtained by attacking German soldiers, since, according to Zanger, the British only armed "white" partisans, who in practice hardly fought at all, and not "red" (communist) partisans.

In 1944, the *Österreichische Freiheitsfront* counted 750 members, and the president of the executive committee was Karl Przibram (b. 21 December 1878, Vienna, d. 10 August 1973, Vienna), who had arrived in Belgium with his wife at the beginning of 1939 with the intention of emigrating to England but was prevented by the German invasion of 1940. After the liberation, Przibram's prestige was so great that he performed the duties of *chargé d'affaires* for Austrian citizens in anticipation of reestablishment of consular and diplomatic authorities..

Irma Schwager, an Austrian antifascist militant from France, writes that she returned to Belgium after the liberation of Paris to help the Austrian antifascist raise the *Österreichische Freiheitsfront*, whose leadership derived from diverse affiliations: social democrats, communists, monarchists and apoliticals.

After the liberation of Belgium, some of the Austrian resistance fighters joined their comrades who had fought in France and who had fled to Switzerland to form a battalion of Austrian partisans in Yugoslavia under the leadership of Max Bair. Four other battalions of partisans were subsequently formed, recruited from among prisoners of war and the *Strafdivision 999* under the leadership of Fürnberg and Honner.

Source (edited): "http://en.wikipedia.org/wiki/%C3%96sterreichische_Freiheitsfront"

1st Belgian Infantry Brigade

The **Belgian 1st Infantry Brigade**, also known as the "Brigade Piron", after its commander, Jean-Baptiste Piron, was a Belgian and Luxembourger army unit which fought in World War II. Within the British 6th Airborne Division, it participated in the Battle of Normandy and, later, the liberation of Belgium and the Netherlands.

Origins

The "Piron Brigade" originated in 1940, with hundreds of Belgian soldiers who had escaped to Britain, as had the Belgian Government. A new command of the Belgian Army, under the command of Lieutenant-General Victor van Strydonck de Burkel, was created in Tenby on 25 May 1940, three days before the Belgian capitulation. Van Strydonk de Burkel became commander of the Belgian Forces of Great Britain in June 1940 and in the same month, a Belgian Minister (Jaspar) called upon all Belgians to come to Britain to continue fighting.

At the end of July 1940 there were 462 men in the Belgian Forces of Great Britain; the arrival of many Belgians allowed the creation of several military units. The troops were trained in Great Britain and Canada and in 1942, Major Jean-Baptiste Piron arrived in Scotland where he quickly joined the Army Staff, with the responsibility of improving the training of Belgian troops. In an artillery competition, the Belgian battery came first. The Belgian Forces in Britain were officially made available to the Allies on 4 June 1942. By the end of the year the army had been restructured, including the creation of the 1st Belgian Brigade, under the command of Major Piron, with a mix of infantry, artillery and reconnaissance units. Troop training continued through 1943 and landing exercises were conducted in early 1944.

A Luxembourger unit was assigned to the "Brigade Piron" in March, forming an artillery troop. Because the Belgians had arrived from around the world, thirty-three languages were spoken in the Brigade in 1944.

Normandy invasion

The D-day landings took place on 6 June 1944 without the Belgian Brigade, to the great disappointment of its 2,200 men, but the British preferred to reserve them for the liberation of Belgium. (This policy was applied to all of the smaller national military units, which were expected to form the core of their post-war armies and for whom it would have been difficult to find replacements for casualties.) Major Piron, however, lobbied the Belgian government in exile, which requested the British Government to send the Belgian troops to the front, to reverse the declining morale of those troops.

On 29 July 1944, the Belgian Brigade was ordered to be ready to move. Its first units arrived in Normandy on 30 July and the main body arrived at Arromanches and Courseulles on 8 August, before the end of the Battle of Normandy. The Brigade operated under the command of the British 6th Airborne Division (Major General Gale), which itself was part of the 1st Canadian Army. The Belgians entered active service on 9 August.

The Belgian Brigade participated in Operation *Paddle* from 17 August with British and Dutch (Prinses Irene Brigade) troops of the 6th Airborne Division. Merville-Franceville-Plage was liberated in the evening, Varaville on 20 August. The Brigade's armoured vehicles were detached to assist British units. Dives-sur-Mer and Cabourg were taken on the morning of 21 August and Houlgate in the afternoon. The Brigade took Villers-sur-Mer and Deauville on 22 August, and Trouville-sur-Mer and Honfleur at the mouth of the Seine on the 24th. The Belgian armoured vehicles were reunited with the rest of the Brigade on 26 August at Foulbec, when the "Piron Brigade" came under command of the British 49th Infantry Division. On 29 August, the Brigade crossed the Seine to support the attack on Le Havre on the following day. At the last moment, however, the Brigade was withdrawn from the front.

The efforts of the "Piron Brigade" on Normandy's Côte Fleurie are commemorated by memorials, road names and war graves.

Belgium and the Netherlands

Instead, on 2 September, the Brigade as well as the Dutch Royal Netherlands Motorized Infantry Brigade was transferred to the 2nd British Army and ordered to move as quickly as possible to the Belgian border. The British Army was already in Belgium and expected to enter Brussels on the following day and this transfer would allow the Belgian and Dutch Brigades to operate in their homelands. The Brigade arrived at the French/Belgian border on 3 September after an overnight journey and continued to Rongy in Brussels the following day, just after the British.

During their advance through Belgium, the Belgian troops were sometimes mistaken for French Canadians, since local people did not expect that their liberators would be fellow Belgians. The Belgian Brigade liberated other Belgian towns and cities before reaching the Netherlands border on 22 September. Its campaign in the Netherlands lasted until 17 November, when it was relieved from the front and moved into reserve in Leuven. The "Piron Brigade" returned to the Netherlands between 11 April 1945 and June 1945.

In the small Dutch border town of Thorn, a bridge has been named in honour of its liberation on 25 September 1944.

Occupation of Germany

The "Brigade Piron" occupied part of the British zone of occupation until 15 December 1945.

Post-war

"Brigade Piron" was the core of the new Belgian Army. In a reorganisation on 17 November 1945, the Brigade's artillery and armoured units were reorganised to form specialised regiments and the engineers joined a newly formed engineers battalion. The remaining infantry, reinforced by volunteers, became the First Brigade Liberation, based at Leopoldsburg (Fr lang: Bourg-Leopold) barracks.

Order of battle

In August, 1944, the 1st Belgian Brigade consisted of:
- Staff
- British Liaison
- 1st, 2nd and 3rd Motorised companies - each with rifle platoons reinforced by mortar, machine gun, anti-tank and anti-aircraft platoons.
- Armoured Car Squadron - 4 squadrons equipped with a mixture of Daimler armoured cars, Staghound armoured cars (some armed with anti-aircraft weapons) and Daimler "Dingo" scout cars and a supply and recovery squadron
- Artillery Battery - 12 25 pounder field guns, organised into 3 troops, one of which was Luxembourgeois.
- Engineers Company
- Transport
- Repair
- Medical Unit

Source (edited): "http://en.wikipedia.org/wiki/1st_Belgian_Infantry_Brigade"

Fort Eben-Emael

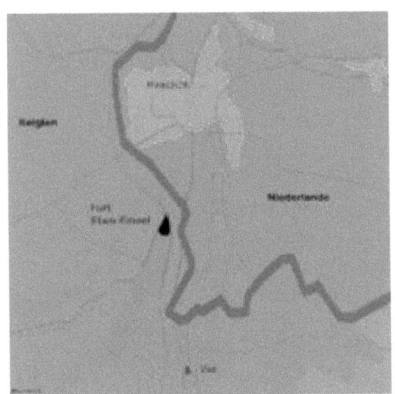

Map of the area between Belgium and the Netherlands near Fort Eben-Emael

A cupola in Fort Eben-Emael after penetration by a shaped charge

Entrance area, July 2007

Fort Eben-Emael is an inactive Belgian fortress located between Liège and Maastricht, on the Belgian-Dutch border, near the Albert Canal, and designed to defend Belgium from a German attack across the narrow belt of Dutch territory in the region. Constructed in 1931–1935, it was reputed to be impregnable and at the time, the largest in the world. The fort was successfully neutralized by glider-borne German troops on 10 May 1940 during the Second World War. The action cleared the way for German ground forces to enter Belgium, unhindered by fire from Eben-Emael. Still the property of the Belgian

Army, the fort has been preserved and may be visited.

Situation

The fort is located along the Albert Canal where it runs through a deep cutting at the junction of the Belgian, Dutch and German borders, about 20 kilometres (12 mi) northeast of Liège. A huge excavation project was carried out in the 1920s to create the Caster cutting through Mount Saint Peter to keep the canal in Belgian territory. This created a natural defensive barrier that was augmented by the fort, at a location that had been recommended by Brialmont in the 19th century. Eben-Emael was the largest of four forts built in the 1930s as the Fortified Position of Liège I (*Position Fortifiée de Liège I* (PFL I)). From north to south, the new forts were Eben-Emael, Fort d'Aubin-Neufchâteau, Fort de Battice and Fort de Tancrémont. Tancrémont and Aubin-Neufchâteau are smaller than Eben-Emael and Battice. Several of the 19th century forts designed by General Henri Alexis Brialmont that encircled Liège were reconstructed and designated PFL II.

A great deal of the fort's excavation work was carried out on the canal side, sheltered from view and a convenient location to load excavated spoil into barges to be taken away economically. The fort's elevation above the canal also allowed for efficient interior drainage, making Eben-Emael drier than many of its sister fortifications.

Description

Fort Eben-Emael was a greatly enlarged development of the original Belgian fortifications designed by General Henri Alexis Brialmont before World War I. Even in its larger form, the fort comprised a relatively compact ensemble of gun turrets and observation posts, surrounded by a defended ditch. This was in contrast with French thinking for the contemporary Maginot Line fortifications, which were based on the dispersed *fort palmé* concept, with no clearly defined perimeter, a lesson learned from the experiences of French and Belgian forts in World War I. The new Belgian forts, while more conservative in design than the French *ouvrages*, included several new features as a result of World War I experience. The gun turrets were less closely grouped. Reinforced concrete was used in place of plain mass concrete, and its placement was done with greater care to avoid weak joints between pours. Ventilation was greatly improved, magazines were deeply buried and protected, and sanitary facilities and general living arrangements for the troops were given careful attention. Eben-Emael and Battice featured 120mm and 75mm guns, giving the fort the ability to bombard targets across a wide area of eastern Liège region.

Eben-Emael occupies a large hill just to the east of Eben-Emael village, bordering the Albert Canal. The irregularly-shaped fort is about 600 metres (2,000 ft) in the east-west dimension, and about 750 metres (2,460 ft) in the north-south dimension. The fort was more heavily armed than any other fort in the PFL I. In contrast to the other forts whose main weapons were in turrets, Eben-Emael's main weapons were divided between turrets and casemates.

- **Block B.I**, entrance block with two 60mm anti-tank guns and machine guns.
- **Blocks B.II, B.IV and B.VI** flanking casemates disposed around the perimeter ditch to take the ditch in enfilade with two 60mm guns and machine guns.
- **Block B.V** similar to II, IV and VI, with one 60mm gun.
- **Cupola 120**, one twin 120mm gun turret. There were also three dummy 120mm turrets.
- **Cupola Nord and Cupola Sud** each had one retractable turret with two 75mm guns.
- **Visé I and II** each house three 75mm guns, as well as a machine gun cloche, facing south.
- **Maastricht I and II** each house three 75mm guns, as well as a machine gun cloche, firing north in the direction of Maastricht.
- **Canal Nord and Sud** were twinned blocks housing 60mm guns and machine guns covering the canal. Sud was demolished when the canal was enlarged.
- **Mi-Nord and Sud** are machine gun blocks (*mitrailleuses*) in the main surface of the fort. They were crucial in defending the top of the fort.

An observation block, equipped with a GFM cloche, overlooks the canal. Underground galleries extend over 4 kilometres (2.5 mi) beneath the hill, connecting the combat blocks and serving the underground barracks, power plant, ammunition magazines and other spaces. Fresh air was obtained from intake vents over the canal.

Personnel

In 1940 Eben-Emael was commanded by Major Jottrand. There were around 1200 Belgian troops stationed at the fort.

1940

On 10 May 1940, 78 paratroopers of the German 7th *Flieger* (later 1st *Fallschirmjäger* Division) landed on the fortress with gliders (type DFS 230), armed with special high explosives to attack the fortress and its guns. Most of the fort's defenses were lightly manned and taken by complete surprise. Much of the fort's defensive armament was destroyed in a few minutes. The attackers were unable to penetrate inside the underground galleries, but the garrison was unable to dislodge them from the surface of the fort. The fortress surrendered one day later, when the German paratroopers were reinforced by the German 151st Infantry Regiment. While 1200 soldiers were authorized to be at the fort on any given day, only 650 were at the fort with an additional 233 soldiers 6 km away at the time of the German assault.

However, the Germans had planned the capture of the fort well in advance. In preparation they had practiced assaulting a full-scale mock up of the fort's exterior in occupied Czechoslovakia using the recently built and captured border fortifications that were modeled to a large degree on western designs. Adolf Hitler himself conceived of a plan to take over the fort by getting men on the fort by using gliders to overcome the problem of concentrating an airdrop on a small target, and utilizing the new top secret shaped charge (also called "hollow charge") bombs to penetrate the cupolas.

75mm turret, B.V

Good espionage and superior planning, combined with unpreparedness on the Belgian side, helped make the execution of Hitler's top secret plan a swift and overwhelming success. The capture of Eben-Emael involved the first utilization of gliders for the initial attack and the first use of hollow charge devices in war. The gliders, led by First Lieutenant Rudolf Witzig, landed on the "roof" of the fortress. There they were able to use the hollow charges to destroy or disable the gun cupolas. They also used a flamethrower against machine guns. The Belgians did destroy one of the key bridges, preventing it from being used by the Germans but also preventing a relieving force from aiding the fortress.

Present day

Fort Eben-Emael is now open for the public to visit. While still military property, it is administered by the Association Fort Eben-Emael, which provides tours and activities.
Source (edited): "http://en.wikipedia.org/wiki/Fort_Eben-Emael"

KW-line

View of bunker H4 and the water duct used to flood the area in front of the tank barricade near the village of Haacht. This is part of the KW-line.

The **KW-line** was the main Belgian line of defence against a possible German armoured invasion through the centre of Belgium, during the initial phase of the Second World War.

The KW-line, also known as the **Dyle-line** (*Dijle-line*) (named after the river Dijle) or **Iron Wall**, was requested by the Belgian Ministry of Defence and built between September 1939 and May 1940. It consisted of a connection of bunkers and barricades between the village of Koningshooikt and the city of Wavre. The barricades were either Cointet-elements connected to each other with steel cables, railway tracks drilled partly into swampy areas, concrete ditches filled with water, or other steel constructions that could hold off armoured vehicle attacks.

In 2009, an inventarisation project was set up. For more details (Dutch), cfr. www.kwlinie.be
Source (edited): "http://en.wikipedia.org/wiki/KW-line"

349th Squadron (Belgium)

The **349th Squadron** is one of the traditional fighter squadron in the Air Component of the Belgian Armed Forces. Originally founded by Belgian refugees in England in 1942 as the 349th Squadron of the Royal Air Force, it was transferred to the Belgian air force in 1946. Considered a 'honorary' squadron, it retained its original name and numbering and has been flying in Belgian colors ever since. Today, it is part of the 10th Tactical Wing and operates F-16 Fighting Falcons from the Kleine Brogel airfield.

History

With the Royal Air Force

349 (Belgian) Squadron was formed as a Royal Air Force squadron by Belgian personal at Ikeja, West Africa on 10 November 1942. The squadron was equipped with the Curtiss Tomahawk for local defence duties. The squadron did not become operational and was disbanded in May 1943. On 5 June 1943 the Squadron was reformed at RAF Wittering with the Supermarine Spitfire V and became operational at RAF Digby in August 1943. The Squadron moved to southern England to operate over France on bomber escorts and low-level sweeps. In early 1944 it began to train as a fighter-bomber unit and then operated in this role in occupied Europe. During the invasion it carried out beach-head patrols and then were used as bomber escorts. In August 1944 the Squadron moved to France in the fighter-bomber role, it carried out armed reconnaissance behind enemy positions and attacked targets of opportunity (mainly vehicles). In February

1945 the Squadron returned to England to convert to the Hawker Tempest. This did not go well and the Squadron regained Spitfire IXs. It moved to Belgium and was disbanded as an RAF unit on 24 October 1946 on transfer to the Belgian Air Force.

Source (edited): "http://en.wikipedia.org/wiki/349th_Squadron_(Belgium)"

350th Squadron (Belgium)

The **350th Squadron** is a fighter squadron in the Air Component of the Belgian Armed Forces. It is part of the 2nd Tactical Wing and operates F-16 Fighting Falcons.

It was formed during the Second World War as **No. 350 (Belgian) Squadron**, passing to Belgium in 1946.

History

With the Royal Air Force

No. 350 Squadron, the first Royal Air Force squadron to be formed by Belgian personnel, was brought into existence in the United Kingdom at RAF Valley in November 1941. The squadron operated the Supermarine Spitfire at first on convoy protection duties over the Irish sea, relocating to RAF Atcham in early 1942. In April 1942 the squadron moved to RAF Debden and carried out offensive operations over France. The squadron moved several times around southern England, in 1944 it provided beach-head patrols during the invasion. In August 1944 the Squadron operated against the V-1 rockets attacking England using the Spitfire XIV. The squadron moved to Belgium in December 1944 to provide offensive patrols over the battlefield including patrols in the Berlin area. The squadron was disbanded on 15 October 1946 on transfer to the Belgian air force.

Source (edited): "http://en.wikipedia.org/wiki/350th_Squadron_(Belgium)"

5th Special Air Service

The **5th Special Air Service** or **5th SAS** was an elite airborne unit during World War II, consisting entirely of Belgian volunteers. It saw action as part of the SAS Brigade in Normandy, Northern France, Belgium, the Netherlands and Germany. Initially trained in sabotage and intelligence gathering, they converted to motorised reconnaissance on armoured jeeps. They were noted for being the first allied unit to set foot onto Belgian soil and the first to cross the Siegfried line. This latter feat although was merely accomplished by accident.

History

A Belgian Independent Parachute Company was officially installed at Malvern Wells (Worcestershire) on the 8th of May 1942 by Mr Henri Rolin, Belgian under-Secretary of Defence. It comprised the following:

1. - A Company 2nd Battalion Belgian Fusiliers, a Battalion mainly made up of volunteers from South and North America assembled since January 1941, who moved to Great Britain in June 1941. "A" Company as a whole had volunteered in February 1942 to train on the lines of an Independent Parachute Company under Lt. Freddy Limbosch as Chief Instructor.

2. - A platoon of the 1st Battalion Belgian Fusiliers with some qualified parachutists (since January 1942).

3. - Volunteers from other units of the Belgian Forces who had escaped from occupied Belgium via France, Spain and Gibraltar.

The newly formed Company continued to train as an Independent Parachute Company making extensive use of the many schools and training facilities offered by the British (the first Parachutists wings worn by Belgians were earned at Ringway parachute school in early 1942). The unit was attached for 3 months to the 8th Parachute Battalion of the 6th Airborne Division in 1943, then spent a month intensive training in December 1943 at the 'Allied Training Centre' Inverlochie Castle (Fort William), and finally moved, in February 1944, to Loudon Castle Camp, near Galston (Ayrshire) to join the Special Air Service (S.A.S.) Brigade.

Like all military units and formations the men came from all walks of life and this was especially true with this particular unit. The volunteers included a former world cycling champion, lawyers, farmers, labourers, lumberjacks, a circus acrobat, a professional wrestler and even three bona fide barons. The commanding officer himself was both a qualified engineer and dentist. The men who volunteered came from all four corners of the world to carry on the fight against the Nazis. Not all of them could even speak the same language. Some spoke French, some spoke Dutch while others spoke only English. These differences of upbringing, class, lifestyle and even language might have seemed problematic but a real esprit de corps developed quickly within the unit.

The role of the Belgian SAS parachutists during the Second World War was primarily sabotage, intelligence gathering and reconnaissance. The men saw their first action towards the end of July 1944 in France. During the Ardennes offensive in 1944 the unit was regrouped and equipped with armoured jeeps. As a reconnaissance squadron, they executed security and reconnaissance missions in order to support the 6th British Airborne Division. In 1945 they were used for counter-intelligence work which involved the location and arrest of top ranking Nazis and war criminals.

In the beginning of April 1945 the Belgian SAS Squadron consisted of three reconnaissance squads which were deployed in the north of Holland and in Germany. After the capitulation of the Germans on the 8th of May 1945 the Belgian SAS participated in 'Counter Intelligence' missions in both Germany and Denmark.

At the end of the war the Belgian SAS Regiment had much to be proud of. They had been the first allied unit to set foot in Belgium & Germany and the only Belgian unit permanently on active deployment between July 1944 and May 1945. They had also been responsible for the capture of Admiral Doenitz's government in Flensburg and the German Foreign minister Von Ribbentrop.

Insignia

SAS pattern parachute wings.

- The cap badge is a downward pointing flaming sword worked in cloth of a Crusader shield. It was designed by Corporal Robert Tait, MM and Bar, of the London Scottish following the usual British Army practice of holding a competition to design the cap badge for a new unit. The competition was held after the close of Operation Crusader. The motto is *Who Dares, Wins*. It was approved by the first Commanding Officer David Stirling, with the proposed wording 'Descend to Defend' or 'Strike and Destroy' disallowed. The sword depicted is King Arthur's Excalibur. Erroneous references to it as the Sword of Damocles derive from an article originally published in the regimental journal *Mars and Minerva*, written by a respected veteran of both British Regiments and the postwar re-raised Regiment. The author was subsequently proved to be incorrect, but the story has been repeated by others.
- The wine red beret.
- The SAS pattern parachute wings were designed by Lieutenant Jock Lewes and based on the basic British Army design approved in 1940 but modified to reflect the Middle East origins of the new unit by the substitution of the stylised sacred Ibis wings of Isis of Egyptian iconography depicted in the décor of Shepheard's Hotel in Cairo.

Disbandment

On the 21st of September 1945 5th SAS was transferred from the British Army to the newly reformed Belgian Army. Renamed the **1st Regiment of Parachutists** they served independently as a highly mobile airborne unit until 1952 when the regiment merged with the Commando Regiment. From 1952 on the traditions of 5th SAS were continued by 1 PARA battalion of the Paracommando Regiment.

In 2011 **1 PARA** and its traditions will be disbanded after 59 years of continuous service. In December 2010 the unit's banner, flag and insignia are taken over by the Special Forces Group

Source (edited): "http://en.wikipedia.org/wiki/5th_Special_Air_Service"

No. 10 (Inter-Allied) Commando

No. 10 (Inter-Allied) Commando was a commando unit of the British Army during the Second World War. The first No. 10 Commando was proposed in August 1940, using volunteers from Northern Command, however there was such a poor response that No. 10 Commando was disbanded and the men that had volunteered were posted to other commando units.

In early 1942 the commando was raised again, this time as No. 10 (Inter-Allied) Commando. By the end of the war the commando had become the largest commando in the British Army and included volunteers from France, Belgium, Holland, Norway, Denmark, Poland and Yugoslavia. There was another group of volunteers in X Troop which contained enemy aliens, Germans and Austrians who had escaped from Nazi Germany. Men from the No. 10 Commando served in the Mediterranean, Scandinavia, Burma and Western Europe during the Second World War, mostly in small numbers attached to other formations, never as a complete unit.

Background

Philippe Kieffer in British uniform with French rank depicted, note the toggle rope around the neck

The commandos were formed in 1940, by the order of Winston Churchill the British Prime Minister. He called for specially trained troops that would "develop a reign of terror down the enemy coast". At first they were a small force of volunteers who carried out small raids against enemy occupied territory, but by 1943 their role had changed into lightly equipped assault Infantry which specialised in spearheading amphibious landings.

The man selected as the overall commander of the force was Admiral Sir Roger Keyes himself a veteran of the landings at Galipoli and the Zeebrugge raid in the First World War. By March 1941 there were 11 battalion sized units now called commandos and each commando would consist of around 390 men in a small headquarters and six troops of three officers and 62 men each.

The idea for a foreign commando unit came from a junior French naval officer, Philippe Kieffer, after he heard of

No. 10 (Inter-Allied) Commando

the successful Lofoten raid. The idea was eventually put to the then Chief of Combined Operations, Admiral Lord Louis Mountbatten who could see the value of a foreign commando unit but insisted it should include volunteers from all the occupied territories.

Formation

Men from No. 6 Polish Troop on exercise in Scotland 1943. Note the No.10 Commando, Poland and the combined operations badges

No. 10 (Inter-Allied) Commando under command Lieutenant Colonel Dudley Lister was formed on 2 July 1942. The men of the new commando were all foreigners except for the British headquarters. Headquarters consisted of a British Commanding Officer, second in command, adjutant, intelligence officer and NCO, medical officer and medical orderlies, signals officer and signals section, training officer, quartermaster, administration officer and drivers. The formation of No. 10 (Inter-Allied) Commando meant that by the end of the war it was the largest commando unit in the British Army. Like all British Commandos the men of No. 10 (Inter Allied) Commando went through the six week intensive commando course at Achnacarry. The course in the Scottish Highlands concentrated on fitness, speed marches, weapons training, map reading, climbing, small boat operations and demolitions both by day and by night. In May 1943 the commando moved to Eastbourne on the Sussex coast where they carried out specialist training which unusually for a non parachute unit included parachute training at No.1 Parachute Training School RAF, Ringway near Manchester (over 80% of the Polish troop were parachute qualified) and they also trained in mountain climbing and Arctic warfare. At the same time as the move to Eastbourne the commando got a new commanding officer when Lieutenant Colonel Peter Laycock took over command on 15 May.

No. 1 French Troop

The No. 1 French Troop was formed in July 1942 By Kieffer, from an intake of 40 Frenchmen, who were initially called 1re Compagnie de Fusiliers Marins (1st Company of Naval Rifles). The unit retained its links with the French Navy wearing naval insignia and headgear.

No. 2 Dutch Troop

The No. 2 Dutch Troop consisted of 62 men under command of Captain Mulders. The troop formed in June 1942 was always below establishment and never deployed as a complete independent unit.But the men acted as liaison officers, guides and interpretors during operations Market Garden, Infatuate I and II

No 3 (X) Troop

The No. 3 (X) Troop was possibly the strangest unit in the British Army, consisting of enemy aliens. Under the command of Captain Hylton-Jones the first men to arrive in July 1942 were eight men from Czechoslovakia. The troop was also known as the English, Jewish or British troop and was officially renamed the Miscellaneous Troop in 1944. Most of the troop had German, Austrian or Eastern European backgrounds, others were political or religious refugees from Nazi Germany,and at least one member had been imprisoned in Dachau and Buchenwald concentration camps. All members of the troop adopted British names and false personnel histories. A total of 130 men served in X Troop, but they never fought as a complete unit but provided valuable service to other formations as interpreters and interrogators. The troop lost 21 men killed and a further 22 wounded, among the highest casualty rate of any British military unit in the war.

No. 4 Belgian Troop

The No. 4 Belgian Troop was formed on 7 August 1942, by seven officers and 100 men from the 1st Independent Belgian Brigade under the command of Captain Danloy. As Belgium had surrendered in 1940, the Belgian forces serving with the Allies risked facing charges of treason on their return; the charges were only annulled in 1948.

No. 5 Norwegian Troop

The No. 5 Norwegian Troop was formed in August 1942 under command Captain Hauge, the men of the troop came from refugees brought back to Britain after commando raids and sailors stranded abroad after the German invasion of Norway.

No. 6 Polish Troop

The No. 6 Polish Troop was first formed in August 1942 as the 1st Independent Commando Company. It was integrated into No. 10 Commando in October 1942. Commanded by Captain Smrokowski is comprised seven officers and 84 men.

No. 7 Mediterranean Troop

The No 7 Troop was formed in May 1943 after a need was identified for Italian speakers. The commander was Captain Coates but difficulties finding Italian speakers in the British Army led to the Special Operations Executive offering Italian speaking Slovenes from the Royal Yugoslavian Army. The troop only numbered two officers and 20 men and it was renamed No. 7 Yugoslavian Troop.

No. 8 French Troop

The No 8 French Troop was formed in 1943 from 45 men of the disbanded 2nd Naval Infantry Battalion which had been stationed in the Lebanon and men who had been interned and released in Spain. The two French troops were combined under command of Kieffer and called the 1er Bn de Fusiliers Marins Commandos (1st Naval Rifles Commando Battalion).

Operations

The men from No. 10 (Inter-Allied)

Commando were usually attached to other units who used their knowledge of the area of operations and the language to their advantage as interpreters and interrogators.

The first action men from the Commando took part in was the raid on Dieppe (Operation Jubilee) on 19 August 1942. Men from No. 3 Troop were tasked with gathering German documents from the town hall and distribute French Francs to the local French resistance. The No. 1 French Troop were attached to No.3 and No. 4 Commando, to act as interpreters gather information and also to persuade Frenchmen to return with them and enlist in the Free French forces. Most of the men from No. 3 Commando were captured during the landings, among the Frenchman attached to them were Sergeant Major Montaillaur who was executed under the Commando Order issued by Adolf Hitler and Corporal Cesar who managed to persuade the Germans he was a French Canadian and eventually escaped and returned to England. The men attached to No. 4 Commando assisted them in the capture of the Hess gun battery, while the men from No. 3 Troop had one killed and two captured and never heard of again.

1943

In early 1943, No. 5 Norwegian Troop worked with No. 12 and No. 14 Commando raiding the Norwegian coast from their base in Lerwick in the Shetland Islands and No. 3 Troop were involved in the Sicily landings (Operation Husky) attached to No. 40 (Royal Marine) Commando and No. 41 (Royal Marine) Commando and later the landings on mainland Italy.

Starting in September a series of raids were carried out, by men from the two French troops and No. 3 Troop, on the French and Low Countries coastlines. These raids under the code names of Operation Hardtack and Operation Tarbrush were for beach reconnaissance, for the purpose of bringing back photographs and examples of mines and obstacles that had been laid. In one of these raids Hungarian born Lieutenant George Lane (real name Dyuri Lányi)

was captured and taken to see Field Marshal Erwin Rommel to be questioned, Lane believed he was not executed under the Commando Order because of his meeting with Rommel. In total 12 men were reported missing during the Hardtack raids and only five were later accounted for. The commando also took over responsibility for small scale parachute operations together with 4 (PARA) Troop, No. 12 Commando in September.

In November No. 4 Belgian and No. 6 Polish Troops joined the 2nd Special Service Brigade in Italy. Notably the Poles captured a German occupied village alone when the 2/6th Battalion Queen's Regiment failed to reach a rendezvous on time. Later in the year No. 2 Dutch Troop was sent to the Far East to work with No. 44 (Royal Marine) Commando and No. 5 Commando behind the Japanese lines in the Arakan in Burma.

1944

In January 1944 the Belgian No. 4 Troop and the Yugoslav No. 7 Troop attached to the 2nd Special Service Brigade were sent to the Adriatic to assist the Yugoslav Partisans. Political differences in the Yugoslav troop and hostility from the partisans led to its disbandment. No. 4 Troop then worked with the Vis Motor Gun Boat flotilla boarding enemy shipping. In April 1944, the commando lost No. 6 Polish Troop which was transferred to the II Polish Corps and later took part in the Polish assault on Monte Cassino.

By the time of the D Day landings the commando had lost the Yugoslav, Polish troops and the two French troops were attached to No. 4 Commando in the 1st Special Service Brigade and landed on Sword Beach. No. 3 Troop was divided by sections between the other eight commando units involved in the landings.

Commandos engaged in house to house fighting with the Germans at Riva Bella, near Ouistreham

The French troops of 185 men in total landed on the left flank of Sword Beach during the second wave, of these only 144 managed to reach the assembly point half a mile inland. Their objective was the Riva Bella Casino in Ouistreham. When they reached the casino the lightly armed French commandos were unable to break into the fortified building and called upon a Sherman tank to assist and soon captured the position. In another sector of the landings Working Corporal Peter Master of No. 3 Troop attached to No. 6 Commando was ordered to walk down the main street of what seemed a deserted village. The intention was to draw fire and identify where the Germans were hiding. By the night of D Day 1st Special Service Brigade, including No. 10 (Inter-Allied) Commando elements had crossed the River Orne and were dug in guarding the left flank of the 6th Airborne Division.

For the next three months No. 3 Troop carried out patrols in advance of the British lines. These patrols were not without loss. The troop commander Captain Bryan Hylton-Jones was captured trying to lead resistance fighters through the lines. Some of the men captured would become prisoners of war while others were never heard of again. Hylton-Jones was later released from captivity by No. 46 (Royal Marine) Commando when they captured a German field hospital at Pont-l'Évêque.

By the time the Allies reached the River Seine the original 185 French troops, had been reduced to only 40 unwounded. The numbers in the French ranks were quickly filled by men who had started training as a new No. 7 French Troop using the number left vacant when the Yugoslav troop was disbanded.

In mid 1944 No. 2 Dutch Troop returned to Europe their first mission on the European mainland was Operation Market Garden 17 September 1944. The troop was divided between the three parachute divisions, 12 men were assigned to 1st British Airborne Division, 11 were assigned to 82nd Airborne Division, Five were assigned to 101st Airborne Division and three were assigned to 1st Airborne Corps headquarters. Another five were assigned to 52nd (Lowland) Division, which was to have been flown into the area when Deelen Airport was captured, eventually they ended up in the Staff of 1st British Airborne Corps.

The Belgian No. 4 Troop had returned to England in June and were selected to capture the French island of Yeu only to find during a reconnaissance that the Germans had already left. They moved to the European mainland and were attached to the 4th Commando Brigade for the amphibious assault on the island of Walcheren (Operation Infatuate).

The assault on Walcheren saw the largest concentration of No. 10 (Inter-Allied) Commando men since their formation parade in 1943. Under command Lieutenant Colonel Laycock the commando was deployed; Headquarters and a section from No. 3 Troop and No. 2 Dutch Troop with Headquarters 4th Commando Brigade. The French No. 2 and No. 8 troops with a section from No. 2 Dutch Troop with No. 4 Commando. While with No. 41 (Royal Marine) Commando were No. 4 Belgian and No. 5 Norwegian Troops. In December the new No. 7 French Troop having completed training joined the other two French Troops still serving with No.4 Commando.

1945

In January to March the three French troops carried out raids on the island of Schouwen-Duiveland to prevent the Germans using the Island to mount operations against Antwerp. In February the Norwegian High Command requested No. 5 Norwegian Troop take part in the Liberation of Norway. The troop was transferred to the Norwegian Army at the end of April and then flown to Sweden dressed as civilians to join the Free Norwegian Brigade which was ready to cross the border if the German garrison refused to surrender.

The next major operation involving men from No. 10 (Inter-Allied) Commando was the crossing of the River Rhine (Operation Plunder) and then crossing the River Weser. The main commando force was 1st Commando Brigade with men from No. 3 Troop attached.

Also in 1945 two new Belgian troops had gone through the commando school and now formed No. 9 and No. 10 Troops. Together with No. 4 Troop they came under command 80th Anti-Aircraft Brigade to provide local security. No. 10 Belgian Troop went onto liberate Neuengamme concentration camp.

Legacy

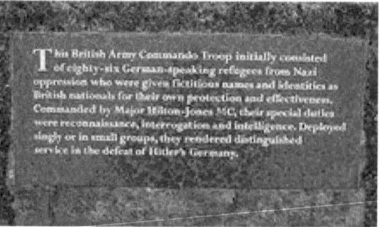

Memorial to the members of No.3 (Jewish) Troop in Penhelig Park, Aberdovey.

After the Second World War No. 10 (Inter-Allied) Commando was disbanded on 4 September 1945, but many of No 3 Troop continued in sensitive and secret work in the occupation zone, tracking Nazi Resistance groups, war criminals and translating captured documents. At the same time the rest of the Army Commandos were also disbanded and the commando role was taken over by the Royal Marines. However the present day Parachute Regiment, Special Air Service and Special Boat Service can all trace their origins to the Army Commandos.

Of the Western nations represented in No. 10 (Inter-Allied) Commando only Norway did not develop a commando force. The French troops are the predecessors of the Naval commandos. The Dutch Troop are the predecessors of the Korps Commandotroepen, and the Belgian Troops are the predecessors of the Paracommando Brigade.

Battle honours

The following Battle honours were awarded to the British Commandos during the Second World War.
Source (edited): "http://en.wikipedia.org/wiki/No._10_(Inter-Allied)_Commando"